The Courage to Lead

The Courage to Lead

ONE MAN'S JOURNEY IN PUBLIC SERVICE

HOWARD N. LEE

Best Wishes to

Wille

Cotton Patch Press, Inc. | Chapel Hill, North Carolina

© 2008 by Howard N. Lee. All rights reserved.
Published by Cotton Patch Press, Inc., Chapel Hill,
North Carolina
Distributed by John F. Blair, Publisher
1406 Plaza Drive, Winston-Salem, NC 27103
1-800-222-9796   www.blairpub.com

Designed and typeset by BW&A Books, Inc.,
Durham, North Carolina
Printed in the United States by Edwards Brothers, Inc.,
Lillington, North Carolina

This book was printed on acid-free, recycled paper meeting the
requirements of the American National Standard for Permanence of
Paper for Printed Library Materials. According to the Environmental
Defense Fund Paper Calculator, using this FSC certified, 30% PCW
paper saved about 42 mature trees.

ISBN-13: 978-0-9816921-0-4
ISBN-10: 0-9816921-0-9
Library of Congress Catalog Number: 2008930637

Frontispiece: 2002 photograph by Will Owens, courtesy of UNC
Chapel Hill Graduate School.

Every effort has been made to find and credit the photographers whose
work adds so much to this book. The photographs by Billy E. Barnes
and Will Owen are published with their permission. If the sources of
other photographs come to light, they will be acknowledged in any
subsequent reprints of this work.

Framed copies of the poems "The Black Man's Journey"
(pp. xii–xiii) and "I Am a Teacher" (pp. 186–187) are available from
Cotton Patch Press, Inc.
109 Glenview Place, Chapel Hill, NC 27514
www.cottonpatchpress.com

To
my wife, Lillian Wesley Lee
my children, Angela, Ricky, and Karin
my grandchildren, Jaimie and Jillian
and
to all the young people who struggle
to find meaning and hope in their daily lives

In memory of
my father, Jesse Joe Howard Lee
my mother, Lou Tempie Barnes Lee
and my grandson, Nicholas

Contents

Acknowledgments

Frank Porter Graham: a special mentor and friend and the individual most responsible for my planting roots in North Carolina

Walter Royal Davis: For being one of my best friends and confidant. And for his encouragement and support

Billy and Anne Barnes

Buie Sewell

Susan Harrison

Chris Minard

Governor James B. Hunt Jr.

Governor Michael F. Easley

Reverend Robert Seymour

William Friday

Maria F. Spaulding

Betsy Warren Harrison

J. Anderson Little

Louise Hall

Marion Ellis

Howard Covington

Joyce Fitchpatrick

Jerry Cooper

Preface

Five years ago I sat down to write my memoir. Frankly, I thought it would be an easy task. After all, I simply needed to recall and write down the facts and chronicle my experiences. It turned out to be the hardest task I have ever undertaken. First, it was difficult remembering events and then positioning the events in the right time frame. Sometimes, reliving some of those times became so painful, I had to walk away and then come back—especially the years spent growing up in the South. During this writing, my emotions ranged from sadness, when I reflected on the early death of my paternal grandmother; anger, when I thought of Little Brother Cooksey and my own treatment upon returning from military service overseas; happiness, when I relived the moments of winning an oratorical contest; and fear, when I remembered leaving the comfort of Savannah, Georgia, and migrating to North Carolina.

But recording this journey has been one of the most therapeutic experiences I have ever had. It has been fascinating recalling and recording how I have grown and matured through the years and just how blessed I have been. In order to capture a snapshot of my life and the meaning I hope it might have for others, I wrote a poem that I believe reflects the spirit of the content of this book. I thank you for being interested enough to read this memoir, and I hope you find some insight in it about your own life and the meaning of your own experiences.

The Black Man's Journey

I symbolize the black man
Who has traveled far.
Who had to walk, couldn't afford a car.
Who bore the whip, its torture and pain.
Who was called boy instead of by name.
Who tilled the soil while his master slept.
Who took his meals at the back door step.
Who was forced to live in a shack out back
Only because his skin was black.
Who survived the oppression of yesteryear,
Still able to laugh while shedding a tear.

I symbolize the black man
Who has traveled far.
Who is no longer walking, now owns a car.
The whip is gone, but not yesteryear's pain.
Who is no longer called boy, but now by his name.
Who doesn't till the soil anymore.
Who now takes meals through the front door.
Who is still struggling to gain full equality,
Yet continues to strive, determined to be free.
Who knows some discrimination of the past is still around,
But is too busy achieving to be kept down.

I symbolize the black man
Who has pledged allegiance to America true.
Who has fought to protect the Red, White, and Blue.
Who has died to preserve freedom and safeguard peace.
Who volunteered and sacrificed to defend democracy.
Who has worked hard and given his best.
Who has become enlightened and passed the test.
Who continues to struggle to gain equal rights.
Who on the backs of ancestors has reached great heights.
Who is finally prepared and is taking his stand,
As a first-class citizen in his American homeland.

I symbolize the black man
Who is not in the place he expected to be,
But who really does want the world to see
That he has overcome, that he has survived,
And in the new age coming, continues to rise.

Howard N. Lee

Howard N. Lee

The first black mayor of a predominantly white community in the South
The first black member of any governor's cabinet in the history of the South
The first black chairman of the North Carolina State Board of Education
A genuine leader

Howard N. Lee's early life in the small community of Lithonia, Georgia, was one of struggle amid extreme prejudice and segregation. The black people in his town, even the teachers and preachers among them, had to be subservient to whites at all times. Lee grew up cautious of white people, trying to avoid being around them as much as he could.

As the grandson of a sharecropper and the son of a man who cleaned railroad coaches for a living, Lee's future looked bleak. At best, he might become a teacher or a preacher or he might get lucky and find work at the post office.

Lee attended the black high school in town that was poorly equipped to prepare him for college, but he went anyway. Determined to be the first black medical doctor to come out of Lithonia, he signed up for pre-med courses at Clark College in Atlanta. If he failed a class, he took it again, and again, persevering for three hard years, until finally it was obvious that this was not the right path for him to follow. He transferred to Fort Valley State College in Georgia, where the president let him enroll on probation. He switched his major to social work and buckled down. He became a student leader and graduated with honors. Drafted into the army, Private Lee organized a sit-in at a drugstore in the Texas town near his base and was punished by being sent to a hardship post in Korea. But even here he showed unusual creative fortitude, becoming a singer in a jazz band and a teacher of English to Koreans.

After his military service, Lee took a job as a juvenile court probation officer in Savannah, Georgia, and this is where his life took two dramatic turns. The first came when he met his future wife, Lillian Wesley Wright, and the second when he attended a lecture one night by Dr. Frank Porter Graham, the former president of the University of North Carolina. Graham promised to help him if he was accepted into graduate school in social work at Chapel Hill. Lee had no idea who Graham was, but he applied, was accepted and, with Graham's help, was awarded a scholarship and access to married students' housing.

Lee was one of only two blacks in his class, but he did not take that as an excuse not to get involved in student affairs; in his first year, Lee was elected vice president of the school's student body, and during his graduation year he was president.

After graduation, Lee was hired to run an experimental program for youth at Duke University. The story of how Lee and his wife found a house for themselves and their children is both chilling and inspiring. Undaunted by displays of resentment and discrimination, they persisted, and with help from some white friends, succeeded in becoming the first black owners of a house in a white Chapel Hill neighborhood.

In another first, Lee became deacon of a predominantly white church in Chapel Hill, where he worked with UNC head basketball coach Dean Smith on an innovative program in local missions. They would become lifelong friends, and later one of Lee's daughters became a member of Smith's support staff. Lillian meanwhile took a job as a teacher with the Chapel Hill school system and was assigned as one of two teachers to develop a school for sick children at North Carolina Memorial Hospital.

After Martin Luther King's death in April 1968, Lee felt called to change society in King's legacy. Lee's frank and detailed account of his life in politics is nothing short of inspiring. When his efforts to have an equal housing ordinance adopted in Chapel Hill failed, he decided he would run for mayor to bring more attention to the problem. He was elected mayor in March 1969, the first black person to become the chief executive of a mostly white community in the South—and he managed to rally support and overcome stiff opposition to pass that equal housing ordinance.

Lee's three successful terms as mayor encouraged him to run for Congress and then for the position of lieutenant governor of North Carolina. Both efforts were unsuccessful, but he attracted enough attention and support to become the first black member of any governor's cabinet in the history of the South. After serving for more than four years as Governor Jim Hunt's Secretary of the North Carolina Department of Natural Resources and Community Development, Lee stepped down to become an entrepreneur, but he missed political life and in 1990 jumped into the fray again when he was chosen to fulfill the remainder of an unexpired term in the North Carolina Senate when the senator resigned.

He was elected to the Senate on his own effort twice, but when he lost a bid for reelection, the new governor, Mike Easley, called upon him to become his senior education cabinet advisor and a board member of the North Carolina State Board of Education, where he was elected chair. Easley was so pleased with Lee's leadership that he also appointed him to serve simultaneously on the North Carolina Utilities Commission. It was another milestone for Lee; he became the first person in history to serve as chair of the state board of education and a member of the utilities commission.

Lee and his wife, Lillian, still live in Chapel Hill, and their story does not end with this inspiring book, for both continue to be very involved in social, economic, and political change.

The Courage to Lead

1 Election Night

On the night of May 6, 1969, my name was written in history. It was unbelievable, but there it was. NBC, CBS, ABC, *Time*, *Look*, and *Ebony* magazines, the *Miami Herald*, the *Denver Post*, the *New York Times*, the *Christian Science Monitor*, even the *Wall Street Journal*, and dozens of other newspapers—all carried the news that Chapel Hill, North Carolina, voters had chosen me as the first black mayor of a predominantly white town in the South. Stories appeared in newspapers in Paris, West Germany, Milan, and all over the world, from places I had never been and in some cases never heard of, and in languages I couldn't read or speak. I was stunned that overnight I had gone from being an invisible person to an international personality.

But I was most proud of the newspaper stories that ran in my home state of Georgia. In my home town—Lithonia, where I was born and grew up—the weekly *Lithonia Observer* ran a story about my candidacy before the election and another story after I won. There were stories in the *Savannah Morning News*, the city where I had worked in the court system. Most special to me was the story that ran in the *Atlanta Journal and Constitution*. The last time my name had appeared in any Atlanta newspaper was when the *Atlanta Journal* listed me as the Best All Round Student in my 1953 graduating class at Lithonia's Bruce Street High School. I had not expected such extensive media coverage of the Chapel Hill election.

My vision of being elected mayor of Chapel Hill had not been very broad. Naively, I had thought it was just a local election. I knew there could be interest across North Carolina, but it did not dawn on me that the nation and the world would care.

Part of the reason for the worldwide news coverage was my background as an unlikely candidate. I had lived in Chapel Hill only four and a half years before running for mayor, and I had little appreciation of the town's national reputation as the home of the fabled University of North Carolina (UNC). Having grown up in Georgia, I knew nothing about Chapel Hill and almost nothing about North Carolina. I had received my bachelor's degree from the tiny all-black Fort Valley State College in Georgia and I had found my way from Savannah to Chapel Hill in 1964 in order to work toward my master's degree in social work at UNC. Up until April 1968, I had had no thoughts or plans to become a political activist, and my wife, Lillian, had made it clear early in our marriage that she didn't want me to seek public office. I had not rubbed shoulders with any famous UNC graduates. I considered myself to be just an average person who expected to live a quiet and unassuming life in one of the neighborhoods of Chapel Hill.

I was, therefore, absolutely surprised when such famous North Carolina alumni as *Wall Street Journal* editor Vermont Royster, CBS *Television News* star Charles Kuralt, *New York Times* national editor Gene Roberts, and other media heavyweights would help propel me to national celebrity status. They obviously delighted in letting the world know that my election was big news and that Chapel Hill had stepped forward and broken a major barrier.

I was pleased that the media portrayed my election as a positive, hopeful sign of racial calming in the wake of riots in several cities following the assassination of Dr. Martin Luther King Jr. thirteen months earlier.

Before we learned the election's outcome, I had been thinking how much fun the campaign had been and that, win or lose, the next day I would go back to work as the employee relations director at Duke University. Everything would return to normal and I would be an invisible individual again. Intellectually, I was prepared to lose, but in my heart I was hoping to win.

By the time Election Day arrived, interest in this Chapel Hill election had superseded any local election in the history of the state. Usually, few people paid any attention to municipal elections, which were generally held in May of odd years. But this night speculation was high that I could become the first black to be elected mayor of a predominantly white southern town in modern times. Reporters from as far away as Greensboro were present. A small crowd had gathered at the campaign headquarters, most of them loyal supporters and campaign workers. There were photographers from the *Durham Herald* and the Raleigh *News and Observer*, as well as from the television stations from Raleigh and Durham. The Chapel Hill radio station was broadcasting live as the votes came in. Suddenly, surprisingly, I was leading by one hundred votes. Even then I expected the lead to evaporate and thought my opponent would ultimately win. But soon, I

Election night in Chapel Hill, 1969, shortly after I was declared winner of the mayoral race.

was leading by almost two hundred votes, then three hundred votes. I was starting to believe the unthinkable might just happen.

As the word spread, people began arriving in droves at the campaign headquarters, until they overflowed into the street. By the time the unthinkable was confirmed, hundreds of people had surrounded the building and blocked the street. One longtime Chapel Hillian said that the outpouring rivaled the night the Tar Heels won the 1957 NCAA basketball championship. Then the announcer spoke the words I had never really expected to hear: "While it is not official, we at WCHL Radio are now predicting that Howard Lee will be elected mayor and become the first black person in the history of Chapel Hill and the state of North Carolina to hold such a high office." I was also shocked to hear that I would be the first black person to be mayor of a predominantly white town in the South. But then I began to feel the weight of the future of the town coming to rest on my shoulders, along with the hopes and dreams of those who had invested their votes in me. I had proposed an ambitious program for Chapel Hill, which included, among many other items, opening the first office for the mayor, starting a public transit system, improving relationships between the town and university, and improving conditions in the depressed areas of Chapel Hill. I was starting to realize I would be expected to do all those things I had promised during the campaign. I remember at one point turning to Lillian and asking, "Now that I've got it, what am I going to do with it?" She responded, "You wanted it, you asked for it, you got it, now it's yours." On the other hand, I was very happy and filled with excitement about the future.

Meanwhile, the crowd had grown too large for the campaign headquarters, so the Reverend Tom Horton of the church next door, St. Joseph AME, offered to open the sanctuary to allow me to address all those who had gathered. I had not prepared an acceptance speech, only one of concession, so I scribbled some notes on a brown paper bag. The church was so full we opened the windows so people outside could hear as well. When Lillian and I walked in, the crowd erupted in applause. It was only the second time in my life I had been given a standing ovation. The first had been when I won a speaking contest in the tenth grade. This time, I delivered a fifteen-minute acceptance speech emphasizing my optimism about the future of Chapel Hill. Two hours of celebrating followed. At the end, Buie Sewell, who had been a driving force behind my deciding to run, arrived. We embraced as he reminded me, "I told you it could be done."

As I have said, I was a most unlikely candidate. I was only thirty-four years old, had never sought or held public office, and had lived in Chapel Hill fewer than five years. It was also inconceivable that a black man could be elected mayor in the South in 1969. In addition, less than 10 percent of Chapel Hill's 12,500 residents were black, and only about half were registered to vote. Then there was another kicker—at the time of the election I worked for the predominantly white Duke University, UNC's fierce athletic rival only nine miles away. During one postelection interview, a dumbfounded Chapel Hill resident said, "I just can't see how we could elect a mayor of Chapel Hill who works for Duke. After all, it's a question of image and pride."

After we returned home that fateful night I called to tell my parents and found them in shock and frightened. My mother kept asking, "You don't think they will assassinate you, do you?" She reminded me that it had been only slightly more than a year since Dr. King had been killed. I assured her that I had plenty of security and protection. (Actually, I had none.) The next morning my parents heard me described on national television as "a person who had risen from the fields of a sharecropper in Georgia to become the mayor of Chapel Hill, North Carolina." We talked again that night, and I was relieved that their fear had been transformed into pride. I must admit that I was also shocked both to see my picture on national news and hear my name spoken on national television.

Time magazine marked my election with a brief article in its May 16, 1969, issue with a headline of "Breakthrough in Chapel Hill." The headline in the *Indianapolis Star* read, "White Southern Town Elects Negro Mayor." The article quoted former Vice-President Hubert Humphrey as saying, "This is a new breakthrough in Southern politics." Humphrey, the Democratic candidate for president who had been defeated by Richard Nixon in November 1968, said in a telegram to me, "These are difficult and challenging times but the willingness of persons like yourself to step forward in the cause of democracy gives all of us new energy and courage. We are proud indeed of what you have accomplished for Chapel Hill and America."

Other telegrams had poured into Chapel Hill, including ones from civil rights leaders and others, such as Coretta Scott King; Roy Wilkins, president of the NAACP; Ralph Abernathy, president of the Southern Christian Leadership Conference; Whitney Young, executive director of the National Urban League; and Congressman John Conyers, the Michigan Democrat. Abernathy included an invitation for me to appear at the SCLC convention in August of that year. Unfortunately, I was not able to accept his invitation, because of official and employment obligations.

"Let me congratulate you on your election," Mrs. King cabled. "You have demonstrated that hard work is always rewarded. I extend to you my best wishes for what I know will be a significant administration in this New South a-coming." I especially treasured her words since her husband had been killed in defense of my rights as an American, including my right to seek public office and live in a decent neighborhood. However, the most important reason I treasured her words was that Dr. King's assassination had planted the seed that led to my eventual run for mayor.

The next day the first national media outlet to contact me requesting an extensive interview was the *Christian Science Monitor*, headquartered in Boston. The reporter, Bill Williams, left a message at my home. When I returned the call, the conversation became almost comical. First of all, he was shocked that I was returning his call in person, rather than through a staff assistant. He asked if he could speak with my press secretary, and I said, "There is no press secretary." He wanted to speak with my executive assistant, to which I replied, "There is no executive assistant." Then he asked if we could meet me at the mayor's office, and I said, "There is no mayor's office." I suggested that we meet at the town municipal building, explaining that my responses would make sense to him when he arrived in Chapel Hill. We met two days later at the municipal building, but instead of doing the interview there I moved it to the College Café on Franklin Street, in the heart of downtown.

I had a special reason for wanting us to go to the College Café. During the month of April 1963, the Student Peace Union had picketed the College Café daily for refusing to serve blacks. It was also targeted by a group called the Committee for Open Business. In spite of protests, the Chapel Hill Board of Aldermen refused to enact a public accommodation ordinance. Things were so contentious that during one daily demonstration in front of the restaurant, the head cook, who was black, quit and joined the picket line. Since there was no one else to cook, the restaurant was unable to serve customers. The owners pledged to serve all customers, regardless of race, if the cook would return to work. He did, and shortly after that the color line was broken. In a short time, other local establishments showed signs of weakening. One was the Pines Restaurant, which had ordered four students, two black and two white, arrested when they refused to leave after being denied service. The Pines was also the scene of a 1964 sit-in by UNC's basketball coach, Dean Smith, along with Dr. Robert Seymour, the senior minister at Binkley Memorial Baptist Church, and a black UNC student. Dean's stance was particularly admirable because he was still relatively new in his job at that time.

When the *Christian Science Monitor* reporter and I arrived at the College Café, we were greeted warmly by one of the owners, who congratulated me on being elected. In addition to this being my first interview with a major national newspaper, it was also the first time I had been to the College Café. Williams and I were seated in a booth in front of a large window facing Franklin Street.

We spent almost two hours together. I explained that Chapel Hill was a council-manager system and that the mayor's role was viewed as being ceremonial. Since all previous mayors had accepted that role, there had never been an office for the mayor. I explained that it was a part-time position that paid one hundred dollars a month, with no vote or veto power, no staff, and no budget. I further explained that the mayor could exert little influence and was only expected to preside at official meetings and cut a few ribbons.

I emphasized that I would not accept this passive role. He thought I had set a high bar for myself and questioned how I planned to reach it. My response was, "I can't tell you now, but contact me at the end of my first year, and it will be done."

Bill's article appeared on May 29, 1969, with the headline, "I'm Walking on a Tightrope . . . ." The first line of the story quoted me pointing out that I would be under intense scrutiny from two extremes—black radicals, who would be expecting me to take up their cause, and white conservatives, who would be watching to see if I actually did. The article continued with another quote from me: "How I perform could have a heavy bearing on the political future of other Negroes. If I do a good job it will pave the way for others to present themselves for office."

The article also quoted me as saying that my being elected mayor was probably not going to set a trend. "But at least it will give some people an opportunity to see a Negro perform in this high office. Also it may open the eyes of those who think all Negroes are militant, destructive, and not law-abiding." I emphasized that it was my ultimate dream that my election would help young blacks believe that preparation and hard work could open many doors.

Looking back on those turbulent times, I see my election as a ray of hope in a dark period punctuated by racial strife and unrest. Chapel Hill itself had not escaped such turmoil. Students had taken over buildings on the university campus in February 1968 and the governor had sent in the highway patrol to quell the disturbance. Stokely Carmichael had visited the campus in late 1968. The black power and black separatist movement, coupled with Vietnam War protests, gave rise to a volatile environment in Chapel Hill. This was just one more obstacle I had to face as I organized my campaign in 1969.

My candidacy as the first black to seek the mayor's office raised hopes that I could be a potential peacemaker. I was not a black militant. I had never been a black separatist. I had always believed that progress could be made through calm and reasoned negotiation, which was Dr. King's philosophy. My attitude, as I grew older and wiser, was to try to work within the system. On this basis, I had the faith and confidence that I could serve as mayor of all the people of Chapel Hill and provide the leadership that could inspire citizens to work together for a better community.

As I savored my election victory, I looked back on my life in wonderment. I was proud to have journeyed from the fields of a sharecropping farm to stand on the threshold of the office of mayor of Chapel Hill, North Carolina. At the same time, I wondered how I would manage the loneliness of public responsibility, as I would need to face two interrelated questions. The first was, how could I grasp the reins of power and exert influence and leadership? While campaigning, I had become painfully aware that all I was inheriting was an important title, some ceremonial trappings, and the symbol of leadership. On the other hand, I had great confidence I could rise up and successfully meet the challenge I had set for myself. I knew that the impact I could make as mayor would result from a blend of my personal convictions, my strength, my determination to change the approach to business, and my persuasive skills. I was convinced then—and am more convinced today—that the quality of a person is much more important than the authority of the position. A person with strong convictions, powers of persuasion, and a clear vision can transform a weak, ceremonial position into a significant role that will gain the respect and confidence of the community, even those who oppose him. A person who is given full authority and great legal powers, but who works to avoid conflict, refuses to take risks, and seeks only to be secure will be useless to himself and others. As a leader, I knew I had to be willing to fail. My second question was, what did I really want to accomplish and how did I want to be remembered when I stepped down from the office? I was most comfortable with what I wanted to accomplish and had clearly articulated that during the campaign.

There is an old Negro spiritual I enjoyed singing, especially the line "My soul looks back and wonders how I got over." I am convinced that what had helped me "over" was the campaign, which included a lot of dedicated people who knew this one-time opportunity had come, would be there for a fleeting time and then would be gone forever, never to return. With that faith, the campaign that we launched was a well-organized and hard-hitting one, unlike any ever run in Chapel Hill.

2 Planting Roots in Chapel Hill

Lillian and I never anticipated that our experience of buying a house in Chapel Hill in 1966 would be such a challenge and eventually lead to my decision to run for mayor. Our plan was to quietly buy a house in a nice section of town, raise our children, and live a comfortable life. Instead we found ourselves engaged in a struggle against discrimination. We were shocked when most realtors in town would escort us to the traditionally black section of town and were hesitant to show us houses in the all-white subdivisions. Chapel Hill was the last place in North Carolina where we expected to receive such treatment. After more than three months of being jerked around, we finally closed on a very nice house located on the east side of Chapel Hill in a subdivision called Colony Woods. Our journey ended in August 1966, when we moved into our house at 504 Tinkerbell Road. But the journey had not been a smooth one.

In March 1966 we had decided to make Chapel Hill our permanent home. In spite of having two job offers—one in Atlanta and the other in Savannah, Georgia—we had grown attached to life in Chapel Hill and felt it would be a good place to raise our family. Lillian had a wonderful job teaching at North Carolina Memorial Hospital and helping develop a school for hospitalized children. We were comfortable with the Chapel Hill school system and felt this would be the best place for our children to get a good education. Once it was known that I would be staying in North Carolina, I was flattered to receive a variety of job offers.

I was really excited, however, when I was invited to interview for a position at Duke University. Never in my wildest dreams could I have imagined being affiliated with such a prestigious southern university in any capacity. I considered it an honor just to be invited for an interview. In March 1965 the Ford Foundation funded a proposal submitted by Duke to develop a comprehensive program of educational intervention in the lives of disadvantaged children from birth through adolescence. The primary focus during the first year had been on assembling staff and developing research assumptions regarding the nature of Durham's disadvantaged children and the best way to serve them. The program was designed to link Duke University, North Carolina College (later North Carolina Central University), the city and county schools, and the local antipoverty agency (Operation Breakthrough).

I studied the goals and objectives of the program and was well prepared for the interview, but I didn't think there was a prayer I would get the job. Having just finished graduate school, with no significant research experience and no publications, I was sure there would be many stronger candidates. I was the last candidate to be called into the interview room. The room was impressively furnished. I was seated at a large table facing three white men, Robert L. Spaulding, Donald J. Stedman, and James J. Gallagher, who were the senior administrators. They explained that the successful candidate would be responsible for developing a program to find ways to intervene to prevent early pregnancies among high-risk adolescents. The interview lasted almost an hour, but it felt more like an eternity. I didn't know what it meant, but I was kept much longer than any of the other candidates. When it was over, I was asked to wait in the reception area. Within fifteen minutes, I was summoned back into the room and offered the job at a starting salary of nine thousand dollars a year, effective July 1966. I was so shocked, I almost fainted. I felt as if I was dreaming and was sure I would wake up and find this was a cruel hoax. But it wasn't a hoax. This was real. I was actually going to work at Duke University.

In August 1966 I was also appointed to the visiting faculty of North Carolina Central University to teach sociology and social psychology.

Two years later, in June 1968, I was asked to join the staff of the vice-president for business at Duke to develop an employee relations program. I spent the next two years working to build trust between the university management and nonfaculty employees.

In January 1970 Dr. William G. Anlyan, vice chancellor for health affairs, recruited me to join his staff and start a program to help low-level hospital employees advance to higher paying jobs. In addition, I was appointed to the medical school staff as a recruiter to help expand the enrollment of black students at Duke.

Although I was proud of the success I had increasing the number of black students in Duke's Medical School, I was most proud of the employee-training program I created, called Path for Employee Progress (PEP). The idea was to find a way to allow low-level workers at Duke—housekeepers, groundskeepers, orderlies, and maintenance staff—to attend the local community college, Durham Technical College, where they would be enrolled in a course of study leading to an associate's degree in a health-related field, qualifying them for such positions as licensed practical nurse or X-ray technician. These opportunities would allow them to begin a path for advancement.

I convinced the administration to pay these employees for a forty-hour work week and to release them for twenty hours to attend classes. Each year one hundred people were chosen. Employees had to apply. They had to demonstrate that they were really committed to following through. Duke supported PEP for the four years I was running the program. So, for the time I was there, four hundred people moved from low-paying jobs to para-professional positions.

One woman, a housekeeper who had fourteen children, not only completed the two-year course to become an LPN but also went on to receive a bachelor's degree at North Carolina Central and become a registered nurse. All the time she was going through this, Duke not only kept her employed but gave her time off to attend classes. She was just one of many who were given this opportunity. I was delighted that Duke committed to this program and stayed the course in support of it. To my knowledge this was the strongest commitment at that time by any institution of higher learning in the state of North Carolina.

The program became so successful that I would travel to other universities and talk about what we had done at Duke, and several other institutions adopted some form of the program. Because Duke made this major commitment to support this program, the employees began to realize that, for the first time, Duke was really making an honest effort to improve working conditions and to provide opportunities for job advancement. I felt that Duke entrusted me with this opportunity. It fit right in with what I have been driven to do all my life, that is, to find ways to inspire and motivate people and help them believe in themselves. I wanted to convince these employees there was no obstacle so great that it couldn't be overcome, and I often used myself as an example of someone who had every reason to lose faith, had every reason to quit, and who just kept finding a reason and a way to keep going and not quit. Not because I was so great but because there was somebody always outside who believed in me and had confidence in me before I had confidence in myself.

Back in 1966, after I had secured my first job at Duke, Lillian and I stepped up our search for a house. Our time was short because we had only thirty days to vacate our student housing apartment. Because we were experiencing such difficulty finding a decent house on which to close, the university extended our stay. We thought it would be an easy task to both locate and buy a house of our choice. But from the outset, we realized that while Chapel Hill enjoyed a liberal image, it was still a very segregated community. After looking at several subdivisions and many houses, we settled on the house we liked in a white part of town.

The real estate agent had always been very courteous and had enthusiastically shown us many houses, both completed and under construction. But a pattern began to emerge. Each time we liked a house or lot and returned the next day ready to make an offer, he would apologize profusely and tell us the property had just been sold. I knew this was the oldest bait-and-switch trick in the book, having watched that process used in Atlanta for years. It was obvious the agent was playing a cat-and-mouse game with us.

We had made and become friends with a white couple, Richard and Joan First, who lived in the Colony Woods subdivision. We shared with them how frustrated we had become working with the realtor. They were able to get the keys to a house that was for sale next door to them. Lillian and I saw it and decided this was the house we should buy. We went to see the realtor and made an offer. He was speechless, then finally said, "I don't think I have a choice. I have to sell you the house." He immediately called his financial partner in Alabama, who requested to talk with me. The partner proposed that if we did not force them to sell to us he would help us buy any house outside his subdivision. I refused and wrote a check for the down payment.

That night I received another call from the Alabama partner, offering again to buy us off—amazingly, trying to make himself the victim. He said, "I just can't believe you're going to do this to me." Somehow he wanted me to believe that *he* was the victim. He said, "You're going to absolutely ruin me. My kids won't be able to go to college, and my wife will be without a nice car. Why would you want to do this to me?" He said, "I'll tell you what I'll do. I'll make a deal with you. If you will go find another house in another section of town, I will not only make the down payment on that house, but I will make your first three months' payments on the house, and I will set up an escrow to pay your taxes on the first year." He said, "I'm told you're an intelligent man, a wonderful man, that you're not a radical like some of the other blacks that are running around, that you would make a good neighbor, but people won't understand that. They will just see you as being black. It's just not the time."

When I said no, there was just silence. Then he said, "Well, what would it take to get you to back away? Name your price." I said, "It won't take anything because I'm not doing it. This is the house we want and we can afford it." I told him that I was personally insulted that he felt he could buy me: "If I were to sell out to you, I could never look myself or my kids in the eyes again. I'm not doing it. We're going to buy the house or we're going to end up in court and you will lose all your financing privileges under Federal Housing Finance and Veteran Administration Mortgage Programs." After that conversation, I never heard from him again and we closed on the house without incident.

The day we moved in, many of the residents came by to welcome us to the neighborhood. There were others, however, who were not very nice. A doctor and his wife across the street immediately erected a "for sale" sign and moved within weeks. The woman would never face our direction. She would back down the driveway to pick up her newspaper and then walk back into the house and never look in the direction of our house. The doctor, on the other hand, was entirely different. On occasion, when she was not around, he would wave. There were a few other residents who were unhappy but did not react outwardly. Other than this one family, no one else moved out of the neighborhood.

Two days after we moved in, I had to go San Francisco to a meeting. While I was out of town, my wife received two telephone calls. One was from a person saying, "If your kids go to school tomorrow, you will not see them tomorrow night." The second call came in before midnight, with someone saying to my wife, "Y'all are trouble makers, so prepare a funeral because your husband won't be coming home alive." The town posted a police guard at the house until I returned home.

The first night I was back home, Lillian and I heard a banging noise near the house. I looked out of the window to see a small cross burning in our yard. At that moment, I had a flashback to Lithonia and the burning cross at the Klan rallies. I was very angry. I bolted out of the door without thinking and proceeded to kick the cross down. I realized later just what a stupid thing that was to do. If this had been a plan to harm us, I would have been an easy target.

The threatening calls continued for weeks, mostly late at night. Eventually a tap was placed on our telephone, and it turned out the calls were coming from a secretary in the real estate agent's office. The agent was quite embarrassed and issued a public apology. Sadly, the secretary was later diagnosed with a mental illness. The cross was erected and burned by a group of neighborhood kids who thought it would be funny to play such a prank. They had no idea as to the seriousness of their behavior. They later confessed that the idea was planted when they overheard some of their parents saying things like, "In the old days, if niggers moved into our neighborhood the Klan would come and burn a cross and that would scare them off." The police were able to find the guilty parties because some of the kids had bragged about it at school. After these incidents, things quieted down.

After we had settled into our house, our attitude was that everything was all right with us, so everything must be all right with the world. Consequently, we withdrew from activism. We felt we had paid our dues when we went out front and integrated the neighborhood. We were still very much involved, but we weren't engaged. So we focused on pursuing more goodies for our urbanized middle-class life and were doing just that the night Dr. King was shot, in April 1968.

We were at Sears and Roebuck, getting ready to buy a clothes dryer, when we walked by a television set and saw the news flash of Dr. King's assassination. The feelings that came over me were like part of my gut had just been ripped out. Suddenly, I was forced to face the fact that everything wasn't all right with the world. Lillian and I decided that buying a dryer was not so important anymore. We left the Sears store and drove home. We were both emotionally shook up, thinking that if this could happen to Martin Luther King, what about the rest of us, who are very much vulnerable? That night I decided that I had to find some way to reconnect, that I could no longer accept the rejection of the Chapel Hill Board of Aldermen to enact an open housing ordinance, that it was not okay for me to live in one part of Chapel Hill when there were blacks in other parts of the town with unpaved streets, rundown houses, and no new construction in that section. It just seemed that the selfishness that had engulfed Lillian and me didn't feel as good as it had before.

Dr. King had made the ultimate sacrifice, and the least I should do was find a way to keep pushing to break down the barriers around me and to help guarantee access for the poorer blacks in Chapel Hill. I realized that I had to find a balance between realistic sacrifice and foolish risk. I couldn't just go out and jump in with a "damn-the-torpedoes" attitude.

Two weeks after King's death, I appeared before the Chapel Hill Board of Aldermen for the second time to ask for an open housing ordinance and was rebuffed again. I left the council chamber that night determined not to let this issue drop again. I started thinking it was about time to take the debate into the political arena. The mayor and three members of the town board would be up for reelection in May of 1969. That night, I decided to turn my attention and energy towards using the electoral process to change the makeup of the board.

I did not believe a black person could be elected mayor in Chapel Hill and thought that it would be tough even for a white liberal. But I reasoned that a friend of mine, Buie Sewell, had a reasonably good chance. He was in his early thirties, tall and slender, with a full head of coal-black, wavy hair. Most women considered him handsome.

Buie had the right image, was well known, and had strong credentials, which I felt would make him an attractive candidate. He was the minister of a predominantly white Presbyterian church, which he had organized and developed. He was the son of a prominent North Carolina politician. His father, Malcolm Sewell, had been North Carolina's attorney general during the Terry Sanford administration in the early sixties.

When I initially proposed the idea to Buie, he seemed excited by it. But as he thought more about it, he liked the idea less. I kept trying to persuade him, but to no avail. My contention was that all we needed to do was hold the three council members we had and get a progressive-thinking mayor who could be a bully pulpit speaker, and then we indeed would have a majority of the council. My sole interest was to get an open housing ordinance passed and I really didn't have any other agenda. I thought that once I talked Buie into running for mayor, we could develop a strong platform. I was absolutely driven just to get this open housing ordinance enacted.

Chapel Hill was a split-personality town. The liberal image was generated from within the university, while the conservatives were the power brokers and businesspeople. Chapel Hill liberals had no power. All political and public offices were dominated by the more conservative element. However, I sensed that the political winds were on the verge of shifting and that 1969 could be the year to have an impact. Students were also beginning to take an interest in the local political process. This shift was being driven by the Vietnam War protest, the civil rights movement, and many problems within the black community that were being ignored by the town.

I reminded Buie that Dr. Reginald Hawkins, a black dentist from Charlotte, had actually gotten the majority of votes in Chapel Hill in the 1968 gubernatorial Democratic primary. I had managed his campaign locally.

Finally Buie said, "Okay, here's the question: other than the open housing ordinance, why else should I run?" I thought for a while and then I said, "Buie, somebody should challenge the other person who is going to run."

I reminded him that the name being thrown around was that of Roland Giduz, a member of the council, a longtime Chapel Hillian and a friend of Sandy McClamroch, the sitting mayor. Roland would be supported by the business community, I said. He had good strong university ties. He was just the perfect candidate to walk right into the mayor's office and do nothing—so why would we want someone at this juncture in our lives to just walk right in without addressing some of the issues? I wanted someone to challenge Giduz because we knew there were many other issues that related to the black community, such as unpaved roads, no sidewalks, and open ditches that were attracting mosquitoes and endangering the health of the residents.

There were no blacks in any major positions in town hall. So I said that we should at least make Giduz discuss his plans to resolve these issues. Buie said, "Yes, but why me? You would make a much better candidate than me. Why don't you run for mayor?" I thought he was kidding, but immediately I could see he was quite serious. I said, "Buie, both of us are intelligent. Chapel Hill is liberal, but you saw what I went through trying to buy a house. Why would you think Chapel Hill would elect me or any other black to be mayor if they are not willing to sell a house to a black person?" He had to admit that was a good point, but he said, "If you just act like you're going to run for mayor, it would probably get a lot of people's attention."

Buie suggested that we bounce the idea off Jim Shumaker, editor of the *Chapel Hill Weekly* newspaper. I reluctantly agreed, but cautioned him not to give him the impression that I had actually made the decision to run for mayor. He said, "No, I will just test it with Jim. He's got a good sense. I will tell him that Ed Caldwell, a member of a prominent black family in Chapel Hill, is also thinking about running for the board of aldermen." I knew that would shake up the black community. Buie called me later in the day and said, "Jim and I had a great conversation." I said, "Buie, Jim's not going to print anything, is he?" And he said that Shumaker promised that he was going to sit on this and that I could rest comfortable. I said, "Buie, can you trust Jim Shumaker?" He said, "Oh, yes." But whatever agreement Buie thought he had with Shumaker became moot when the next issue of the paper came out. My candidacy was the top headline, which read "Black to Run for Mayor," with my picture plastered on the front page.

The news hit Chapel Hill like a wildfire going through dry brush. I showed up at a Christmas party and was bombarded with questions from both sides. One side thought my candidacy was a terrific idea, and the other side was saying, "You have got to be some kind of idiot. You don't really think Chapel Hill is going to elect a black mayor in 1969?"

This is where the whole process began to take on a life of its own. I had to admit that getting all this attention and knowing that it was creating a little bit of unrest in Chapel Hill gave me a bit of a rush. So for the first time, I let myself really begin to think about the prospect of sticking my toe in the political water, just to see how it would feel. But I had two problems now that the news had hit the street. I needed to talk with my superiors at Duke—and convince my wife.

I had a little problem at home. Before Lillian and I were married, back in Savannah, Georgia, she had made it very clear to me that she didn't like politics and would never get involved, no matter what I decided to do. She even tried to get me to promise that I would never run for public office. At that time I saw no prospects that I would ever have the chance to seek public office anyway. But, fortunately, I never got around to making that promise.

When I finally talked to Lillian, she said, "You're going to ruin everything we've worked for. You could end up losing your job at Duke. You need to remember we just bought this house, and we've got two children to educate." I tried placating her by pointing out that I would just test the water. She eventually agreed, and said, "Okay, I'll go along with it for now, but don't get me wrong. I'm not agreeing for you to run for mayor. Sending a message is one thing, but running for office is more serious."

I discussed with Lillian the idea of pulling together a small group to brainstorm about my running and, to my surprise, she agreed. I then approached Anne and Billy Barnes, who had been friends for four years and who were also fellow members of Binkley Baptist Church. Anne had been a community organizer and was engaged in Democratic Party activities. Billy headed the public relations operations for the North Carolina Fund, which was an antipoverty program started by Governor Terry Sanford. They both immediately agreed to attend and preside at a small group meeting. Anne and Billy would later agree to become my campaign managers.

In mid-January 1969, we scheduled a meeting for a small, carefully selected group. In addition to Anne, Billy, and Buie, other invitees would consist of major black leaders, as well as people who had worked in local campaigns for Eugene McCarthy, Robert Kennedy, and Reginald Hawkins. One key person was David Ethridge, an incumbent member of the Board of Aldermen and son of retired publisher Mark Ethridge of the *Louisville Courier-Journal and Times*. David, who had come to North Carolina to

publish a statewide financial journal, was one of the first people to as-
semble a liberal political organization to work in political campaigns and
especially to elect liberals to local offices. David himself had been elected
in 1967 and was one of three liberals on the six-member Chapel Hill Board
of Aldermen. The other two were Mary Prothro, the wife of a progressive UNC professor, and Reginald D. Smith, a black educator and a well-
respected community leader. David was initially cool towards the idea of
my running for mayor, but got on board once he was convinced it just
might be possible to pull off a win.

As the word circulated that I was calling a strategy meeting to discuss
running for mayor of Chapel Hill, the floodgates opened. We had a list of
fifteen people we had designated to be invited to that first meeting. But
that night we had throngs of people show up who had not been invited. Of
course, planning a campaign, we were not about to turn anybody away. We
ended up having to cram at least fifty people into the basement of the house
we had bought on Tinkerbell Road.

So that night I stood up and presented a list of issues that needed to be
addressed in the campaign, and then I said I was the person who could
carry this message into a campaign as mayor. When I opened up the floor
for discussion, people had all kinds of questions. "How are you going to
work full-time and run for mayor?" "Do you really think people in Chapel
Hill will vote for someone who works for Duke University?" "Some of the
black power advocates will try to defeat you because they will think you
will be an Uncle Tom." Then Alden Lind, a liberal UNC political science
professor and a staunch Democrat, said, "I really just don't think the time
is right. We need to establish relationships with someone who has a chance
of being elected mayor." Irritated, I said, "Alden, all my life I have heard
the words 'the time is just not right.' You've just convinced me that's why I
should run."

There were still some who felt my chances of winning were slim and that
such a campaign would only aggravate and alienate the power structure.
However, the overall sentiment was one of encouragement. During the
next weeks, I talked with university professors, students, and some business leaders. The black leadership also wanted to have a special meeting to
discuss their feelings. Mrs. Rebecca Clark invited a group of black leaders
to talk with me, one of whom was Hilliard Caldwell, a prominent Chapel
Hill civil rights leader. The discussion was honest and direct about senti-
ments towards me among blacks. Some resented that I lived in an all-white
subdivision on the east side of town. Many were concerned about my being

a member of the "white" Binkley Baptist Church because they felt it might appear that I had abandoned the black church community. There was even concern about my being affiliated with Duke University. I explained that I considered myself a pioneer, breaking down barriers in each of these cases. I pointed to the many problems that had been ignored in Chapel Hill, which I would work to solve if elected mayor. Hilliard Caldwell was the most vocal as he urged me to think about running for a seat on the Board of Aldermen rather than for mayor. He was not convinced that even if I was elected I could carry out any of the promises I would make. In the end, I said, "If I don't run for mayor, I will not run for anything." When the meeting was over I had very little support and only a commitment by those in attendance to keep an open mind.

When I left this meeting, in spite of the lack of enthusiasm, I had decided I would definitely become a candidate for mayor. The next step was to meet with Anne, Billy, and Buie to make campaign plans. From that meeting we formed a campaign steering committee and made plans to launch the campaign.

3 The Campaign for Mayor

On February 29, 1969, I opened a campaign headquarters and officially announced my candidacy for mayor. This was a first. No mayoral candidate had ever opened a campaign headquarters, and no campaign had been kicked off with such fanfare. The news media didn't bother to cover the event, because many believed I had no chance of winning. There had been many failed attempts to wrest power from the status quo leaders. Consequently, most of the public offices were occupied by white men, except for one woman, Mary Prothro, and one black man, Reginald D. Smith, on the Chapel Hill Board of Aldermen, and one woman, Betty June Hayes, who was the Orange County register of deeds.

There was no question that if it became obvious I might be elected, the establishment power brokers would pull out all stops to maintain control of the mayor's office. Therefore, my campaign strategy had to be centered on building a strong coalition among blacks (who comprised less than 12 percent of the total voting population), university professors, students, and young progressives like me who were new to the area. While I wasn't optimistic that I could get significant support from the moderate to conservative segments of Chapel Hill or even within the business community, I wanted to make a special effort to reach out and at least lessen their opposition. The veteran incumbent mayor, Roland "Sandy" McClamroch, owner of the local radio station, had not announced whether he would seek reelection. Sandy was a very moderate and popular mayor and many who eventually joined my campaign would not have abandoned Sandy to support me. Fortunately, in early February 1969 he announced that he would not seek reelection. Speculation was that his childhood friend Roland Giduz would become the establishment candidate. Giduz, a longtime university employee, enjoyed a positive image in Chapel Hill as a progressive, and it was known that he expected to be the next mayor.

However, I was more optimistic about my possible success after Sandy announced his decision. Not long after, rumors began circulating that Gi-

The official opening of the campaign headquarters for the mayoral race, 1969. Flanked by my wife Lillian Lee (left) and Alderman Reginald D. Smith (immediate right).

duz himself might decide not to run. For a while, some speculated that I might not have any opposition. I never believed that and continued to prepare for a hard and serious campaign. I believed the stars were aligned and that the time was right for building a strong and active coalition that could change the political landscape in Chapel Hill and Orange County. On February 24 Roland Giduz issued a simple statement, without fanfare, declaring his candidacy, and filed for the office of mayor. While I felt Sandy would have been impossible to beat, I did not view a campaign with Giduz to be a cakewalk. Giduz had it all going for him. He had been a member of the town governing board for twelve years. He was a native of Chapel Hill. His father had been a highly respected professor at the university. He had a majority of the business community's support. He was viewed as a Chapel Hill progressive and had a reputation of being responsive to the black community. He had been one of the calming voices during the early civil rights years, having condemned egregious behavior exhibited by some townspeople, especially those who had poured Clorox on demonstrators and the woman who had urinated on the head of a demonstrator at a local restaurant. While I was starting with a small group of outside supporters, Giduz began with a vast majority of the residential vote.

I had lived in Chapel Hill fewer than five years and had no experience of being elected to or serving in any public office. I was, moreover, employed by Duke University, so some thought it would be terrible to elect a mayor affiliated with the "opposition." This was shaping up to be a classic challenge of "black, inexperienced newcomer against well-known Old Chapel Hill native." At one point some joked, "It's Duke against Carolina."

When asked why I was really running, I responded, "I want to force discussion of important issues that need to be addressed by the town and force commitments to fix them, regardless of which of us is elected." In the face of this huge hill I had to climb, that was the only way to keep myself focused and optimistic.

I started my campaign for mayor knowing I had to overcome two likely objections to my candidacy: my political inexperience and my skin color. To change people's minds I had to personally reach as many people as possible. I knew I had good ideas about what needed to be done and I had the oratorical skills to express my plans. In order to achieve this goal, we arranged for Lillian and me, both jointly and individually, to attend neighborhood coffees and receptions. During the course of the campaign, Lillian and I went to well over 150 events and met with more than 2,000 voters. In mid-March, we unveiled another facet of the campaign by producing and distributing "Lee for Mayor" lapel buttons, bumper stickers, matchbook covers, posters, and a slick brochure. Giduz was caught off guard but quickly recovered by producing his own brochure and distributing other campaign materials. Within a week after my campaign headquarters opened, Giduz opened his. Each time he thought he understood our strategy, we would unveil another. I then began campaigning from a travel trailer, with a "Lee for Mayor" banner on it, which was parked on Franklin Street.

In April the Chapel Hill chapter of the North Carolina Jaycees invited Giduz and me to make a joint appearance at its monthly meeting. Giduz immediately accepted, but I was hesitant, thinking I would be walking into a crowd stacked against me. We decided it would make sense for me to go and give it my best shot.

When I arrived at the meeting, I could sense that my suspicion was right. While I was treated courteously, most of those in attendance were paying more attention to Giduz. It was clear: I was not considered a serious contender. It had been determined that I would speak first, which I was delighted to do. I gave my speech laying out what I would achieve if elected mayor. Giduz, however, was not a very effective speaker and did not offer any plans for what he would do as mayor. During the question-and-answer period, I responded to every question, whereas Giduz was evasive. When the meeting was over, it was clear that Giduz had lost most of his support. I was amazed at the complete shift in attitudes by those attending the meeting. As I left the meeting, I was told by more than one attendee that he had arrived supporting Giduz but was leaving supporting me. I felt energized but realized that this was a small group and I needed to keep working hard.

The last person to talk with me that night was Joseph Nassif. Joe paid me the ultimate compliment by saying, "You so impressed me with your exciting plans for Chapel Hill, I really want to be a part of your administration." The next day Joseph filed to run for the municipal board and was subsequently elected.

Following that meeting, I decided to send a letter to all Chapel Hill voters emphasizing my commitment as mayor to "preserve the best and change the rest of Chapel Hill." In that letter, I talked about how we should not destroy the good things that had occurred in Chapel Hill but should be prepared to take bold action and make changes for improvements. A major plank in my platform was a commitment to establish a public transportation system. There was an expressed need for a bus system in Chapel Hill, but little action had been taken to develop one. The university contracted with a private bus company to operate between various parts of the campus and downtown, but that was all. I proposed to take the plunge and initiate a more extensive town-wide system if elected. Even some of my strongest supporters thought that such a promise was too ambitious and could be used to profile me as a "big spender" mayor. I was quite comfortable with that and decided to rise or fall pushing that issue. I felt that average voters would recognize the advantages of a public transit system, which would encourage the university to adopt policies limiting the number of cars students could bring to Chapel Hill. I justified my proposal on the basis that the town was heading towards a massive traffic problem unless it had some alternative transportation plan. Parking was already creating major headaches for both the university and the town. Chapel Hill didn't have parking garages, and students were taking up all the available spaces. Even neighborhoods near campus were being impacted by the increased number of cars on the streets. The downtown merchants were sold on my proposal because they wanted some way to ensure that customers could have access to their stores. They felt they were losing business. Beyond promising a transit system, I also promised to expand parking for downtown.

My platform included several other measures to improve the quality of life for everyone in Chapel Hill. I had a plan to expand affordable housing, especially public housing. I committed to aggressively apply for federal funds to finance programs to redevelop depressed and blighted areas, which were occupied mostly by blacks. I also made a commitment to expand and upgrade the community recreation program and facilities.

Other services were deficient and needed attention. The university owned the water system and depended on one source, University Lake, to supply water for both the institution and the community. Consequently, for several consecutive summers Chapel Hill had experienced a serious water shortage. There was no doubt, Chapel Hill was a fast-growing community and on the verge of a serious crisis. Therefore, I pledged to create a water resources commission that would be charged with developing long-range plans to expand water sources. The university also owned all the utilities services, which included the local telephone and electric services. Both systems were in serious need of upgrade. I pledged to find a way to encourage the university to sell the utilities services to the town of Chapel Hill.

I felt the local minimum wage was inadequate and that Chapel Hill had not been aggressive in recruiting new job sources. I promised a serious industry recruitment program to bring in new businesses, and to work to improve town and university relations by creating a town-gown commission.

I was encouraged I could attract votes from among the Jaycee organization specifically and the business community in general. During the last month running up to the election, Lillian and I continued our aggressive neighborhood campaigning. We met hundreds of voters in small groups in various homes with great success. I recruited and invited high school and university students to become actively involved in my campaign. In return I promised to appoint young people to serve on many mayoral appointed committees and commissions. University students were at the headquarters most evenings calling voters and distributing literature in neighborhoods. This was the first time the university campus, students, and faculty had become this involved in a local campaign. Even elementary school children were passing out flyers in their own neighborhoods.

This had already become the most expensive local campaign in the history of Chapel Hill and the county of Orange, breaking all spending records when it exceeded five thousand dollars. Most contributions were in small amounts: nickels, dimes, quarters, and dollars. To meet the campaign budget, I made personal loans to the campaign, and several friends cosigned bank loans.

I was not surprised when rumors started to circulate that my campaign was being financed by civil rights organizations such as the Student Non-Violent Coordinating Committee, the NAACP, and the Congress for Racial Equality. Of course, nothing was further from the truth. I purposely did not receive and chose not to solicit out-of-town contributions.

In spite of these rumors, I felt good about my chances of winning. I needed a strong black voter turnout and still worried about whether the voters would turn out in large numbers on Election Day. But I was comforted by the active involvement of Mrs. Rebecca Clark, Hilliard Caldwell, and other community leaders, who had fully committed themselves to get out the vote. The last few days before Election Day, I chose to spend most of the money on hard-hitting newspaper and radio advertisements.

Some of the black leaders were suspicious that the power brokers would begin passing money around to buy the black vote. However, there was no indication that such an attempt was in the works, until a prominent local minister was observed riding around the black community with Mayor Sandy McClamroch. The black leaders focused on closing the ranks and intensifying efforts to discourage any vote selling.

On Election Day, May 6, I was confident we had positioned ourselves to win, yet I was still not sure we would win. Throughout the day, my emotions ebbed and flowed between confidence and doubt. There were workers and watchers at all polling places. Voters were called throughout the day, and vehicles were constantly dispatched to take voters to their polling places and back home. One local businessman, George Harris, owned a black Rolls Royce. We offered rides to the polls in the Rolls. At one point people started calling indicating they wanted to go to the polls but would only go if the Rolls took them. The late Doug Clark, of the rock group Doug Clark and the Hot Nuts, canceled an appearance and allowed his bus to be driven through neighborhoods picking up anybody who had not voted and taking them to the polls. These two vehicles attracted the most attention. We did run into one problem. Those who had gone to the polling place in the Rolls wanted to be taken home in the Rolls. Instead, we returned most of them home on the bus. Needless to say, some were not happy.

A black waiter took the day off without pay to work the polls. Students, both high school and university, rushed from class to help at the headquarters or work the polls. That morning the university student newspaper, the

Daily Tar Heel, had come out with a resounding endorsement of me. This type of endorsement had never happened before in a local race. This was the same *Daily Tar Heel* in which coeditor Gary Blanchard, in 1963, had written, "That may be important, that civil rights stuff, but it's not our issue. It's not something we need to worry about." The newspaper's endorsement in 1969 set a precedent and underlined the significance of this day.

That night we all gathered at campaign headquarters to wait for the returns. The first precinct to report was the upscale Country Club precinct, which gave Giduz a 245 to 115 lead. My heart sank, and I imagined this would be the trend. But then, to my surprise, the tide turned dramatically. From that point on, I carried not only the two majority-black precincts, but two large, all-white precincts as well. By 9 P.M. it was over. Blacks and whites were running into the street, making V signs, and horns were blowing as people yelled: "He's done it! Howard Lee has done it!"

In the middle of all the celebrating, Roland Giduz came to my headquarters to congratulate me. He was, as he had been throughout the campaign, a gentleman. I have always appreciated him for never raising race as a part of his campaign. He later stated to the press, "On that day, the better candidate won."

Later that night, when Lillian and I were finally alone, I was able to admit how unprepared I felt for the challenge. This was the first time the awesome responsibility of being mayor created in me a feeling of loneliness. I had made a lot of big promises I had to keep. But, more importantly, I realized that the hopes and dreams of many rested on my shoulders. I understood that many, especially blacks, expected me to right all the wrongs and to correct all the neglect heaped on them through the years. Yet I also realized the need to keep a proper balance and never make decisions based solely on race. As Lillian and I lay in bed trying to grasp the meaning of how our lives would be changed forever, I began replaying my life as it had developed in Lithonia. I felt that all the experiences of growing up on a sharecropper's farm in the South had prepared me for this new journey and propelled me to this position of power. I was ready to get started.

4 My Family and the Farm

I was born on July 28, 1934, on a sharecropper's farm on the outskirts of Lithonia, Georgia. In March 1932, my grandfather Walter Homer Lee relocated the family (his wife Minnie, their two daughters, Louise and Nevada, and one son, Howard, who would be my father) to a farm of approximately one hundred acres owned by a Mr. Johnny Sills. My grandfather, who had dreams of owning his own farm, had been sharecropping a small farm in Rockdale County, Georgia. Mr. Sills persuaded my grandfather that if he would work the farm for five years, he could live rent free and would have the right of first refusal if the farm was sold. In exchange Mr. Sills would underwrite all operating expenses and they would split any profits fifty-fifty. In addition, Mr. Sills would receive one pig a year slaughtered, dressed, and cured; one frying chicken a month, dressed; and one gallon of milk, one dozen eggs, and one pound of butter each week. My grandfather eagerly accepted the offer and felt this might be the chance for him to ultimately fulfill his dream of owning a farm.

The farm needed a lot of work to clear the land and prepare the fields for planting. On the other hand, the farmhouse was in good shape. This was the largest house the family had ever occupied. It consisted of four bedrooms, a living room, a kitchen, and a screened back porch. There was a large barn, which housed two mules and a horse named Charlie and several milk cows. There was a small flock of chickens.

Shortly after the family settled in on the farm, their son, Howard, announced his intentions to marry Lou Tempie Barnes. This caught my grandparents by surprise, since there had been no indication he was even thinking of marriage. After all, he was apparently enjoying being one of the area's most eligible bachelors and was pursued by many ladies. He was over six feet tall, brown-skinned, with curly black hair, and resembled his mother. My grandmother was apparently quite pleased with his choice of wife and, according to her, was very relieved he had not chosen from among some of the others who were in pursuit. My parents were married

The wedding picture of Lee's father and mother, Howard and Lou Tempie Lee, October 1933.

in October 1933, a few days after my mother's twenty-fifth birthday. My mother moved to the farm from Rockdale County, where she had lived with her maternal grandmother, Lula Hamm, since she was five years old. The family pitched in, worked hard, and had a very successful first year. My grandfather Homer made enough money that year to buy his first car, a used 1929 A-Model Ford. In November my mother announced that she was expecting a baby. The family was elated and started making plans for my arrival—the first grandchild.

Immediately after I was born, my grandmother Minnie retrieved a sterling silver spoon and a small gold ring with a ruby inset, my birthstone, from a box that she kept locked and stored in a trunk. She told me how she had saved enough money during the nine months of my mother's pregnancy to purchase the ring and spoon. She put the ring on my finger and the spoon in my mouth, simultaneously expressing with pride, "I wanted this to be the first black baby born in Georgia with a silver spoon in his mouth and a gold ring on his finger."

I know this because when I was six years old, she told me about what she had done. She also told me that my aunt Louise had leaned over me and said, "You can grow up and be a special person. Someday you might be a congressman or a senator." I often think of her prediction and am amazed how it came true. Aunt Louise was hoping to be a successful pianist. Sadly, I never got to know her and she never got to fulfill her dream. Aunt Louise died six months after I was born from complications resulting from an appendectomy.

The following year, on September 29, 1935, my brother Minnard Louis was born. My father wanted to name him Joe Louis in honor of the heavy-weight champion. But my grandfather Homer and several relatives thought that whites, especially Klan members, would interpret this as an arrogant gesture since Joe Louis was beating up on so many white fighters. Joe Louis was viewed by whites with great disdain. They were determined to prevent the rise of another black fighter like Jack Johnson. My father eventually compromised on the name Minnard, but insisted on keeping Louis as his middle name. My father never gave up on the name he wanted. Until his death he always referred to Minnard by the nickname "Joe."

Minnard and I thoroughly enjoyed our life on the farm. I consider those to be among the best and happiest years of my life. Besides each other, our constant companions were the horse, and two hound dogs, Mutt and Jeff. While our parents worked in the fields during the day, Minnard and I would be left on a blanket to be watched over by the dogs.

My grandparents were strong, optimistic, and determined people. My grandfather would often tell me, "Son, tomorrow can be better than today. But sometimes life will knock you to your knees. When it does, just get up, dust yourself off, and keep moving."

My grandmother Minnie was a very strong and determined woman. I remember her as the dominant source of strength in our family while I was growing up. I always referred to her as "Mamma," and when she spoke everybody listened, including my grandfather. She was a strikingly beauti-ful woman, almost six feet tall, with distinctive features as a result of being the child of a half-black, half-Indian mother and a white father. She never talked much about her parents. When I would probe to try to learn more about them, she would simply promise to tell me some day.

I recall how confusing it was for me when her only first cousin, Sally Jones, who lived in Atlanta, would visit. She was very light-skinned. She actually looked white, with blond hair and blue eyes. On one occasion, after one of her visits, my grandmother overheard me telling one of my broth-

Lee as a baby, born on the farm, with his paternal grandmother, Minnie Brown Lee.

ers, "She is our white cousin." Grandmother Minnie became very agitated and told me she was not white and I should never say that again. Later she explained that her father was a white man. He owned the farm where she and her cousin grew up. She told me that their mothers were half-sisters, that the white farmer was father to both her and her cousin: they were not only cousins, they were also half-sisters. I was totally confused and did not really understand her message until I was much older. From that day until she died, my grandmother never discussed the subject again. I have always been grateful that she shared at least that part of my history with me.

My grandfather Homer, on the other hand, was of pure African descent. He was the oldest of seven children: five boys and two girls. His mother, Leola, lived to be over one hundred years old, but his father, Joe Lee, died in his fifties. After their father died, Homer's four brothers quit farming, moved to Lithonia, and took jobs at a rock-grinding factory known as Big Ledge, a quarrying operation owned by a family by the name of Davidson.

Homer had little formal education, having quit school in the fourth grade. However, he taught himself to read and write functionally. He felt it was imperative that I take full advantage of school and obtain a good education. At the same time, he believed it equally important to develop a strong work ethic. I remember him assigning me, when I was just five years old, such chores as feeding the chickens. I recall how driven and determined he was to own land and be a successful farmer. He expected my father, his only son and the youngest of four children, to play a major role helping develop the Sills farm into a successful venture. My father was an obedient son, but he did not have the same passion for farming as my grandfather.

My father was convinced that farm life would not be in his, or the family's, long-term best interest. Both my parents shared these feelings but did not want to abandon my grandfather and dash his dreams of possibly buying the farm. My mother was taking correspondence courses, hoping to someday teach. On the other hand, my father knew the only decent job available to him would be at the Big Ledge Quarry. Like his father, he had quit school after the fourth grade and was only functionally literate. My father had a very quick temper and on more than one occasion got into fights. I recall one fight when he cut a fellow on the arm so badly he almost died. After that my father realized how close he had come to being

Lee at four years old, living on a sharecropping farm.

imprisoned and began controlling his temper and avoided fighting. He also enjoyed alcohol, mostly "moonshine," but he drank only on Friday and Saturday nights.

My mother, Lou Tempie, was an only child, born October 16, 1907, in Conyers, Georgia. Her parents separated when she was five years old. Her mother, Maggie Hamm Barnes, decided in 1912 to move to Birmingham, Alabama, as a live-in servant with a white family. So at five years old my mother was left with her maternal grandmother, Lula Hamm. Maggie had promised to return for her daughter within six months but, unfortunately, that never happened. Consequently, my mother was raised by and lived with her grandmother until she married my father. I don't recall ever speaking to or seeing my grandmother Maggie in person. In November 1942, thirty-two years after she had left home, Maggie died in Birmingham of a rare disease. My mother brought her home and laid her to rest in the family cemetery near Conyers, Georgia.

My maternal grandfather, Charlie Rother Barnes, had meanwhile remained in the area but only visited my mother sporadically. He was apparently known as a fun-loving man who enjoyed the company of many women and indulged in heavy drinking (though again, on the weekends only). He, too, had a very quick temper, which eventually got him into serious trouble. The story is that he had a heated disagreement with a white man about the amount of money he was owed for work. Supposedly, the man called him a "lying cheating nigger" and kicked him on the leg. Charlie retaliated by punching him in the face, causing him to fall backwards, and he apparently hit his head on a rock. Thinking he had killed him, Charlie, with the help of friends, fled the state of Georgia. This incident took place in 1913. It turned out the man did not die, but Charlie did not know this until many years later. It made no difference that the man survived; Charlie knew that retaliating as he did was enough to get him killed. When he left, he knew he could never return to Georgia.

By mid-1936 my mother and father had decided they wanted to leave the farm and find a house of their own. By now it was clear that Mr. Sills did not really intend to sell my grandfather Homer the farm. More importantly, my father felt he needed a more reliable source of income than the farm, and my mother wanted to substitute teach while working to earn her high school diploma. While looking for a place to rent, my father heard about an older lady, a Mrs. Anna Darden, who was looking to sell her house on Swift Street in Lithonia. My grandfather agreed to the purchase, but the sale was contingent on allowing Mrs. Darden to live in the house rent-free until her death.

In September 1936 my parents left the farm and moved into the Darden house. The plan was for both Minnard and me to move with our parents, but my grandmother Minnie insisted that I stay on the farm. Actually, I preferred to remain on the farm rather than leave my dog and horse. For the next six years, living with my grandparents gave me deep connections to them both—connections that shaped my growing sense of self.

My father began working at the Big Ledge Quarry, and my mother started substitute teaching. In April 1937, my mother gave birth to her third child, another boy, who was named Walter Rother, the first names of each grandfather. The family was beginning to wonder if there would ever be a girl. Then, in December 1938, my mother gave birth to her fourth child— a girl. My grandmother Minnie insisted that she be named Louise in memory of our aunt who had died in 1934.

By the time I was five years old, in 1939, I could read and solve basic math problems. My mother, who was now teaching first grade in a rural one-room school, decided to enroll me as a first-grader. At the end of the school year, when all other students were being promoted, my mother held me back. I was devastated. Her rationale was that while I had the best grades in the class, I had worked only hard enough to stay a little ahead. She was convinced that just getting by was not good enough. Therefore, she was not going to reward me for mediocrity. That is a lesson I have never forgotten. Since that experience, I have always tried to do my very best, regardless of the outcome.

The next year I was sent to Lithonia Colored School in town and repeated the first grade. Each day, my grandfather would drive me to school in the morning and pick me up in the afternoon. My teacher, Mrs. Richardson, had been told by my mother to push me hard and make sure I did my best. The competition was stiffer in my new school, and Mrs. Richardson was tougher. I had learned my lesson and made sure I performed at the highest level. It paid off. At the end of the school year, I was among the top five performers in the class and was promoted to the second grade with the blessings of both my teacher and my mentor mother.

One of the saddest feelings I can recall was watching my grandfather lose his enthusiasm and his drive to continue working to expand the farm. He really wanted to leave, but he had nowhere to go. Instead, he agreed to take care of the farm animals and work just fifty acres of the farm. He and Mr. Sills started a joint venture business, contracting to raise pigs for individuals and deliver them prepared for storage. My grandmother Minnie contracted to do weekly laundry and provide sewing services for well-to-do whites. She made and sold hundreds of dresses and quilts during this time. My grandfather told me they made more money providing these services than they did when they were farming full-time.

But, in spring 1942, my grandfather and Mr. Sills had a major disagreement over an amount of money my grandfather felt he was owed. Unable to resolve their differences, my grandfather decided it was time to leave the farm. When my grandfather broke the news to the family, I was devastated. My grandfather announced we would move into the Darden house with my mother and father. I had felt we would be on the farm forever, which had been the only home I had known. More than anything else, I was really heartbroken when I learned I would have to leave the horse, Charlie, who I thought was mine. I remember begging my grandfather to buy him from Mr. Sills and was told that even if Mr. Sills would sell him, which he doubted, there would be no place to keep Charlie at the Darden house. I was allowed to take my dog, Jeff, and Minnard was allowed his dog, Mutt. Mr. Sills and my grandfather agreed that he could take one milk cow, one hog, and six chickens.

I have always thought that the last few days we were on the farm, Charlie sensed we would be leaving each other. Whenever we were together, he would playfully bump me with his nose and follow me around the farmyard. When that fateful day arrived, we all packed in the car and headed out. As we drove away, Charlie trotted to the end of the fence and watched as we drove out of sight. Occasionally, Mr. Sills would allow my grandfather to take me back to visit Charlie, which would always be a grand reunion. But over time the visits became less and less frequent, until they just simply faded away. One sad day, three years after we left the farm, Mr. Sills came to tell my grandfather that Charlie had died of old age.

So the four of us—my grandparents, Aunt Nevada, and me—moved into the three-room Darden house with my parents, my three siblings, and Mrs. Darden. Instead of improving our living conditions, I felt we had gone backwards. Not only was the house small, the land around it was only one half acre, and it seemed tiny in comparison to the spaciousness of the farm. In addition to the three rooms, two sleeping rooms, and a kitchen, there was a screened-in porch area, which housed an indoor well. This area was used as a family eating space in the warm months but was not usable in the winter. Just outside the back door, there was a smokehouse constructed of rock, which was used to cure pork. The house was located on a major paved highway, the main route to Augusta, Georgia. There was a busy railroad line on the other side of the highway. We had neighbors on the west side, and a large noisy sawmill on the east side of the house.

Even at eight years old, I realized this living arrangement was not at all good; it was, in fact, very uncomfortable. Yet I also understood that this was the only option available to us. So we all settled in to make the best of a bad situation. My aunt Nevada slept in one room with Mrs. Darden, while the rest of the family—my parents, grandparents, and the three of us children—all slept in the second room. The only other room in the house was the kitchen, which we shared with Mrs. Darden. For two years, ten of us occupied this house, until Mrs. Darden died in 1944. In spite of the cramped conditions, the family kept growing, as my mother was pregnant with her fifth child, my brother Frankie. By 1946 the family had nevertheless saved enough money to become the first family on our street to install electric lights and a two-party-line telephone system.

After Mrs. Darden died, my aunt moved her bed to the kitchen area, where she slept until the family was able to construct a room to serve as a kitchen in later years. The rest of us continued to occupy the one bedroom. The adults slept in the two beds in the one room, while the five of us children slept on pallets.

My grandmother worked at a dress-making factory as a seamstress until she lost her sight in 1945. She was not well enough to work but was not

The three-room house in which Lee lived and grew up, Swift Street, Lithonia, Georgia. Parked in the drive is my first car—a 1961 Chevy Impala.

bedridden. However, shortly after electricity was installed in the house, she was struck by an electrical spark caused by lightning striking the house. Looking back, I am convinced she had diabetes, which seemed to run in the family, but it is also my belief that the lightning strike hastened her death. On the day of her death in 1948 at age fifty-eight, I kissed her good-bye as I did each day and went off to school. That afternoon, as I was on my way home, the kid who lived next door rushed to tell me, "Your grand-mamma died." I frankly thought he was teasing and went home expecting to find her well and sitting in her usual chair. Unfortunately, when I walked in the house, I knew immediately that she really had died. All the customary signs were there. Her bed was stripped, the mattress was folded over, and all the mirrors in the house were covered. Then I asked, "Where is Mamma?" My father replied, "She just up and left us." I was emotional and upset that no one had come to get us from school and was told, "I guess we just forgot about you." My parents never knew just how much that statement hurt.

I struggled for weeks before I finally accepted my grandmother's death. I wondered if I would have felt better if her death had been expected. Losing my grandmother was like losing a part of me. She was by far the person who was most my inspiration, my heart, and my soul. She was the one person who had the greatest impact in shaping me as a person. She was also the one who gave me my sense of self-worth and a true understanding of the meaning of determination. For years after her death, whenever I experienced adversity, I always felt my grandmother Minnie was there by my side. Experiencing that loss prepared me to meet and survive tough times and tough challenges.

Shortly after my grandmother's death, my mother gave birth to my second sister, Annie Lois. Then, in 1952, my youngest brother, Larry, was born. My mother almost died from complications of Larry's birth and was hospitalized for weeks following it. This was also the year my father decided he would quit his job at the rock quarry. He felt that with a family of seven children, he needed a safer and better paying job. Fortunately, he was hired as a coach car cleaner by the Georgia Railroad Company. When he quit the quarry, the owners warned that if he lost his new job, they would not rehire him. At the same time, he was criticized by many of his cousins for walking away from the quarry and turning his back on the Davidson family, who had been so good to him. Even my mother questioned whether he was making the right decision. But my dad worked for the railroad company for approximately thirteen years before he was laid off. Then he worked in

Howard Lee's paternal grandfather, Walter Homer Lee.

the X-ray department at Emory University, where he stayed until he retired in 1975.

My grandfather Homer lived with us for only one year after my grandmother's death, during which time he met and married his new wife, Henrietta. He moved into Henrietta's house and lived with her there until his death. My grandfather was truly my hero and my most influential role model. He was a strong, take-charge leader and a mesmerizing speaker. Growing up, I would watch him rise in church and hold the audience spellbound while he spoke. He was so good I thought he should have been a preacher and one day asked why he was not one. His response was indicative of his wise counsel. He said, "Son, I don't want to be like some of these boys who think they can preach. God tells us to go *hear* a preacher and we mistakenly think he said go *be* a preacher. That's why we have so many jacklegs who think they can preach." On occasion, when someone has made a similar suggestion to me, I think of my grandfather's words.

After he remarried, my grandfather Homer went in 1949 to work for a company, for the first time in my memory. He operated a weaving machine at the Porterdale Cotton Mill near Covington, Georgia. Because there were many people living in Lithonia who worked at the mill, they were transported the ten miles by bus five days a week. He was the only black person among them. But during these five years, he sat in the same seat in the middle of the bus without any problem. Then a new white man was hired who decided he wanted my grandfather to sit in the back of the bus. My grandfather refused to move and was supported by the bus driver. This fellow, who was believed to be a Klansman, threatened to have my grandfather "put in his place." This was a frightening time, since my grandfather worked the 3 P.M. to 11 P.M. shift and had to walk a half mile to get home. We all understood this would be a perfect time for harm to be done. Consequently, my father and three of his uncles formed a posse. They would take turns, and each night two of them would meet the bus, armed, and drive my grandfather home. This went on for about a year, until my grandfather decided to retire. I was very proud of my grandfather for holding his ground. I always respected him as a man, but because of that stance he became a giant in my sight.

After his retirement, my grandfather lived a quiet life at home. Each day he would walk the two miles from his house to our family home. He was extremely proud that he had lived to see me graduate from high school and attend college. He often talked about how proud my grandmother Minnie would have been of my accomplishments. He also reminded me of the pressures of being the oldest and my needing to set examples for my siblings. On occasion he would refer to the fact that we shared a common link—of both being the oldest of seven children.

In early 1955 he was diagnosed with high blood pressure, but the doctor felt it could be controlled with medication. He was doing well and had just celebrated his seventy-first birthday. But then, on Saturday morning, June 11, he uncharacteristically called to say he didn't feel well and would I come sit with him while his wife was at work. I got to his house about 8 A.M. and found him in bed. As the day went on, he showed signs of feeling better and even ate a cup of soup. I remember that day as the best I had ever spent with my grandfather. Among the many things we talked about that day, he told me how proud he was of what I was trying to achieve. His final words to me were, "Son, someday I know you will be very successful. I want you to work hard and do well." I didn't want to disappoint him, so I never told him that I was not accepted in summer school and that I was on the verge of being kicked out of college. He talked about some of his disappointments in life, but also his blessings. He was especially proud of his grandchildren. He was disappointed he never owned his farm, but he was proud he was the one in the auditorium when I won "that speaking contest." At 5 P.M., after his wife, Henrietta, arrived, I went home, expecting to see him the next day. The next morning at 7 A.M. Henrietta called to say he had collapsed. He was pronounced dead on Sunday morning, June 12.

Once again, I felt as if a stake had been driven into my heart. My grandfather was the second most influential person in my life. His imprint is so strong that even today when I make a speech I occasionally hear my grandfather's wisdom influencing my words.

After my grandfather's death, my mother and father were shocked to learn they were the beneficiaries of a large sum of money from an insurance policy he had kept active. My parents used the money to enlarge the house, building one room for the four of us boys, and a kitchen. This was the first time we had any semblance of privacy and the first time we boys could sleep in a bed.

I have sometimes wondered how my parents and grandparents had the strength to keep going, facing so much pressure, uncertainty, and disappointment. But then I realize this is what has given me and my siblings our strength.

We have enjoyed levels of success beyond our expectations. We have established our lives in the spirit of our parents and grandparents. All of my brothers and sisters have remained within fifty miles of the home place. I am the only one to have left the state of Georgia. My brother Minnard returned to Lithonia after two years in the U.S. Army and retired after over twenty-five years at the Lithonia Lighting Plant. My second brother, Walter R., retired from the VA Hospital in Atlanta and now lives in Conyers. My sister Louise became an accomplished musician, following in our mother's footsteps, and retired after over thirty years teaching in the Dekalb County public schools. My fourth brother, Frankie W., retired from the Dekalb County school system after more than twenty-five years there as an administrator. My second sister, Annie Lois, retired from the Lithonia Lighting Plant after more than twenty-five years of service. My fifth brother, Larry Barnes, retired after twenty-five years of employment with a utility company. I am convinced that our success has resulted from our earlier experiences and the tight-knit bond of love that has kept us together through the years.

Occasionally, I think of the days on the farm and realize it was that experience that contributed greatly to my survival skills and my success. It was on the farm that I grew as a young boy and developed strong self-esteem and self-confidence. It was on this farm that I raised my first watermelon and tasted the sweet joy of success. It was on this farm that I developed my work ethic and concluded that the wealthiest people were the ones with access to food, a happy family, good friends, and above all, strong character. All this contributed to making me ready to begin the new experience of growing up in Lithonia.

5 Growing Up In Lithonia

Growing up in Lithonia was not easy during the 1940s and 1950s. It was a small town in the middle of Georgia, dominated by huge granite quarries, a town where segregation was the accepted order of life. Lithonia was General William Sherman's first night's stop on his march from Atlanta to the sea at Savannah in 1864. The home he stayed in is still standing. His troops burned the railroad depot but spared the Masonic lodge hall, which also still stands. Lithonia was only eighteen miles east of Atlanta, but it might as well have been a thousand. The town had fewer than two thousand people, about half of them black.

The town was named in the 1840s when a local teacher combined the Greek word *litho*, meaning rock, with *onis*, meaning place. Rock so dominated the Lithonia landscape, it was difficult for the mostly small business owners and farmers to clear enough area to plant crops. But by 1880 most had come to realize the potential wealth of the community was its vast supply of granite. Around 1880 the tools were invented that made it possible to quarry the granite for commercial purposes. Between 1890 and 1920, Lithonia was enjoying great success built around this booming granite industry. After weathering the Depression, Lithonia became a thriving small town attracting skilled stonecutters from Scotland, Ireland, and Wales. During the 1940s and 1950s, unlike surrounding towns, Lithonia was able to make many infrastructure improvements such as paved roads and sidewalks, lighted streets, a civic center, parks and swimming pools, a health center, and a library. Of course, all were segregated and for "whites only." Main Street was a busy center of commerce, with mercantile stores, hardware stores, drugstores, restaurants, and a movie theater. People commuted from long distances to work at the Big Ledge Quarry. The name "Lithonia" and all the rock the town was named for were appropriate emblems for that part of my life because to me it always felt like growing up between a rock and a hard place.

The main source of employment and the town's wealth, the Big Ledge

Quarry, was located on the north edge of town. This was the site of the major part of the vein of granite, which ran six miles north to the famous Stone Mountain. The Davidson family, which owned the quarry, dominated the town, and just as in the movie *Gone with the Wind*, their mansion on Main Street was a principal landmark. It was the perfect picture of the southern plantation house, with its four tall, white columns. No blacks were ever allowed to walk through the front door. It was accepted practice that blacks and working whites always went to the back door of the Davidson mansion. Of course, blacks were always expected to proceed to the back door of any dwelling occupied by whites.

The quarry jobs were considered the best ones in town, but they were dirty, dangerous, and unhealthy due to all the dust that would accumulate in workers' lungs. Most of my relatives were employed there. Unfortunately, too many relatives worked there until they were too ill to work any longer, and ultimately died at young ages because they had inhaled the dust and developed silicosis.

Violence against blacks was commonplace in Georgia in those years, with murders and lynchings being reported in the press regularly. Lithonia was no exception. These flames of racism were fanned across Georgia by a racist governor named Eugene Talmadge. He always made race a central focus of his campaigns. In his final campaign, he challenged white men to stand firm with him "and keep these niggers in their place." Talmadge died in 1946, just before taking office for his fourth term. Blacks cheered and celebrated throughout Georgia. Students in classrooms shouted for joy. However, some of the older teachers chastised us for celebrating death. They pointed out it was bad manners and disrespectful to cheer when someone died, even if it was a "bad" person. This was a moment used by our teacher to impress on us to always celebrate life, not rejoice in death. Still, I could not help but feel glad he was dead.

My grandfather certainly did not hide his attitude and was quite vocal about how he felt. He went so far as to proclaim he wanted to go to his funeral, just to make sure that Talmadge was the one in the casket and that he was really dead. But more than anything else, I learned from this event that "no one monkey stops a show." In Georgia the governor changed, but the conditions and the rhetoric remained the same.

Ku Klux Klan rallies were a frequent occurrence in Lithonia. Every Friday afternoon, droves of Klansmen would parade through town in cars and pickup trucks, waving guns as an intimidation tactic aimed at keeping blacks in their place. At the end of the parade, the hooded figures would gather a few blocks east of the center of town in a vacant field near our house on Swift Street. They would listen to hate speeches that would whip the crowd into a high emotional state. The rally always ended with the burning of a gigantic, gasoline-soaked cross. Occasionally, we would hear that some black person had been attacked and beaten during the late hours. Sometimes they would just plant and burn a small cross in somebody's yard as a warning.

In the late forties things began to change in Lithonia as young black men began to exhibit rebellious behavior and an unwillingness to behave subserviently as expected by whites. This attitude was fueled by black soldiers returning to Lithonia from the Second World War. They had fought for democracy in foreign countries and did not understand why they had to come home and be treated as second-class citizens. Their attitude was, "If we can fight the enemy overseas, why should we tolerate the harassment of the Klan at home?"

As these black soldiers began returning home, they exhibited a boldness that whites had not seen before in Lithonia. Several soldiers made threats about organizing and fighting the Klan. A few made it known that killing a few "crackers" would be just as easy as killing Germans. These comments made both white and black leaders in town very nervous. There was no precedent set where former soldiers had encouraged others to rise up and fight against the Jim Crow system. The threats certainly heightened tensions in town. My father and grandfather were so uneasy they kept loaded shotguns locked in a closet. On one occasion I overheard my grandfather saying to my father, "Son, if these crackers decide to start lynching Negroes, we need to be ready to take a few with us." As a young boy, I was both nervous and excited at the same time. I did feel some comfort that my parents were ready to die fighting to protect us. Eventually, cooler heads prevailed, and as the talk of insurrection subsided, tension was reduced.

Willie "Little Brother" Cooksey was one of those who returned home after spending several years overseas. He had been wounded in battle and had received many medals of honor. Little Brother, like most black kids, did not graduate from high school. Therefore, the only jobs available to him were either in construction or at the Big Ledge Rock Quarry. He was not at all quiet about his resentment of being unable to get a decent job, especially after fighting in the U.S. Army. He was also bitter because his younger brother had been killed in combat.

But just as things were calming down, the stuff really hit the fan again. The word spread around town that while Little Brother was working with a construction crew near a small grocery store, a white girl walked by the work site. He made a wolf whistle and then loudly bragged about how many white girls he had slept with overseas. This boldness stunned both black and white members of the crew. Later that day, he was fired, and was reminded about what happens to "niggers" who even look at a white woman. He just laughed as he left the construction site. The black workers watched in silence as he casually walked away with a smirk on his face.

Little Brother was last seen alive when he left a social gathering just after midnight. The next morning his body, having been run over by a train during the night, was found on the railroad tracks near our house. My grandfather, who was one of the local undertakers, helped collect the mutilated body. Against my parents' advice, I watched in horror as Little Brother's body was placed in a huge basket. It was later determined that his head had been split open with an ax and his body placed on the tracks, obviously to cover what had actually happened. Nobody ever really spoke the words, but we all thought this was the work of the Klan.

My grandfather was not gentle with me that day as he hammered away about Little Brother and why I needed to always keep control over my emotions. His advice was, "Son, someday things will change. Someday the bottom rail will rise to the top. Someday, if you live long enough, you will be a free man. Someday these white folks will get their foot off our necks because they can't keep us down without staying down with us. Someday somebody will rise up and say enough is enough. I probably won't live long enough to see it happen, but if you are smart you may live to see it. You can be a part of making things change—if you can survive. But you can't help anybody if you are dead. Son, be smart not stupid."

Both my father and grandfather insisted that I should understand the difference between resisting and learning how to survive without putting myself in danger. I listened to their words, but they were not registering. I told them that I thought it was cowardly not to stand up and resist being oppressed. I will never forget the expression on my grandfather's face as I said that. He looked me directly in the eyes, put his hand on my shoulder, and said, "Son, if you remember nothing else, remember this. It would be better to be a coward for a few minutes than become a corpse forever." I heard his words and understood the message he was trying to give to me. I have never forgotten my grandfather's words, and years later they would serve as a reminder not to be stupid. What he said to me that day has continued to serve as a calming effect in my life.

There is no question the future was bleak, but I was too innocent and naive to believe it. All blacks in the town were kept in subservient roles, even the teachers and preachers.

Lithonia had only one doctor, who was white. He did treat blacks, but only after he treated all the whites. Even if a black had an emergency, whites were always served first. The entrance for blacks was through a side door to the waiting area in an unfinished basement. Fortunately, I had to go to the doctor only once, for treatment of a wound that required stitches. I had been running barefoot, trying to retrieve one of our pet rabbits, which had escaped. I stepped on a piece of broken glass and cut my foot to the bone. Ordinarily, an injury would have been treated at home, but my parents realized stitches would be required. My dad took me to the doctor, who put in six stitches, using only alcohol on the wound to dull the pain. My dad had to hold me down while the doctor stitched. I had never before and have never since felt such excruciating pain.

I viewed whites as symbols of the economic success that I dreamed I could enjoy one day myself. They owned the businesses, lived in the big houses, and drove the nice cars. In my mind, I felt I wanted to be like them. But most of my role models were black.

Besides my father and grandfather, another man who played a pivotal role in helping shape my life was the master of my Boy Scout troop, Mr. Lucius Sanders. Upon returning to Lithonia after the war, Mr. Sanders decided not to challenge the status quo but to find ways to positively impact the lives of black boys. Consequently, he organized the first black Boy Scout troop in town. My brother Minnard and I were very excited about joining. Unfortunately, most parents, like ours, could not afford to pay the initiation fee and buy uniforms and equipment. Mr. Sanders therefore raised money from various sources and equipped all of us boys who did not have the resources. I viewed Mr. Sanders as someone special, and we all viewed him as a hero. Every week for two years he dedicated his life, energy, and time teaching us survival skills. His influence on the lives of all of us in the scout troop contributed to our insight and understanding of life. Although he had fought in the war, he always preached that violence was the worst way to settle disputes. He was truly a role model for me.

There was one other black man who stood out as a role model and who symbolized the image of success that I wanted to achieve. He was the only black man I knew who carried a briefcase and wore a suit and tie during the week. His name was John Wesley Dobbs, a postal clerk who had carved out a leadership role among Atlanta's black elite by leading voter reforms and pushing for the hiring of Atlanta's first black policemen. When I was growing up, Mr. Dobbs was being called "the mayor of Auburn Avenue," the main street in black Atlanta.

"Mr. John Wesley," as he was sometimes called, supplemented his income by selling insurance. My mother was a client, so he would make frequent visits to our house to collect premiums and discuss the affairs of the day. He always carried himself with dignity and grace and drove a nice car. He had six daughters, including the famous opera singer Mattiwilda Dobbs. One of his grandsons, Maynard Jackson, grew up to become the first black mayor of Atlanta. I wanted to be like Mr. Dobbs someday, but I had no clue of how to go about it. Yet his image and his modeling has been a driving force throughout my life. It is ironic that in 1972, during my second term as mayor of Chapel Hill, North Carolina, I was asked to help Maynard Jackson in his first campaign for mayor of Atlanta. It was then I learned that Mr. Dobbs was Maynard's grandfather. I could not help but think how I was in a position to help the grandson of the man who had so inspired me.

Growing up, I did a lot of walking and spent a lot of time alone because most of the black kids would tease me and say that I took life too seriously. I didn't play and joke around a lot. I read a lot of books, especially comic books. I also spent a lot of time listening to such radio shows as *The Shadow, Amos and Andy, Lum and Abner,* and *Sky King.* I'd rather be listening to the radio or reading a book than be out playing marbles. Most of the black kids did not enjoy reading and often accused me of being too studious. In spite of the oppressive times, I still made myself believe things could be better someday.

This optimism was based, in part, on the fact that one of my good friends and frequent playmates was a white boy named Lukee. Lukee and I had hung out together since we were ten years old. We lived in the same general neighborhood, but we connected mostly because we both enjoyed reading and trading comic books. We would meet and spend hours together at least twice a week. We were aware of racial problems and differences, but we were too busy having fun and enjoying each other's company to be swayed. In spite of racial segregation, it was acceptable for black and white kids to play together up to a certain age. We both had friends within our race, but we seemed to have more in common with each other. Yet, subconsciously, we both knew that things would change someday.

As Lukee and I grew older, we both started to talk about segregation and why whites and blacks didn't seem to "get along." Since we got along so well, we found it difficult to understand why adults had such difficulty getting along with each other. We never found an answer to our question and most of time we avoided focusing on the subject too long. I think that deep inside we knew and were concerned that someday we might have to separate because of our skin color, and we just didn't want to face the possibility. I believe we found it less painful not to think about the future and instead concentrate on the present for as long as we could. But then it happened in the fall of 1949, following our fifteenth birthdays, that our friendship abruptly took an ugly turn. Although we still liked each other and enjoyed each other's company and friendship, the racial wall became a reality.

One brisk fall Saturday morning, as Lukee and I met to trade comic books, I noticed he was not his usual jovial self and seemed unusually sub-dued. This felt really strange because Lukee was always happy and talka-tive. I thought he might have had a fight with his parents or that he might have been ill. As I was methodically examining each book, he kept urging me to hurry up and decide. His pushiness was starting to annoy me. Fi-nally, I said, "You don't seem right today. You OK?" He looked at me in silence for a few seconds and then confessed that his father had told him that he couldn't play with me anymore and that he never wanted to see us together again. He confessed that his dad had told him that the neighbors didn't like me hanging around their house and that self-respecting whites did not associate with "niggers."

I was absolutely stunned. But I was even more stunned when he went on to tell me that his father had told him that it was time for him to be-gin thinking about joining the Ku Klux Klan. Amazed, I asked, although I already knew the answer, if his father was a member of the Klan. He dropped his head and in a soft, somewhat embarrassed, voice said, "Yeah." The shocking part was that his father had always been nice to me and had never shown an attitude of prejudice. Nothing in his behavior pattern indi-cated to me that he was a bigot. It was hard for me to believe that my friend and his family could have such prejudiced attitudes.

I asked Lukee if he planned to join the Klan and he said he didn't know for sure, but he didn't think he had any choice. "After all," he said, "I am white and my father said that any white man worth anything will work to keep niggers in their place." I asked, "Do you really believe that?" He replied, "I don't know what I believe. I just know I can't hang around with you no more." I could tell that he was becoming agitated at me asking so many questions. "Well," I said, "I guess we won't be exchanging comic books anymore." "I guess," he said. He began gathering his books to leave, but then paused, looked at me, and said, "I'm sorry but this is the way things have to be. My daddy said this is the natural order. He said that we have to keep you in your place and never let you all think you're as good as white folks." He was now starting to chap my hide, as I felt myself growing angry. I couldn't believe that anybody could change so quickly. I felt as if I was having a bad dream. The fact that, in less than a week, a person with whom I had spent so much time was now telling me that he had to keep me in "my place"—this was both unacceptable and was never going to happen. As he walked away, I said, "Lukee, don't you ever mess with me. Don't ever try to keep me down. Don't ever come after me. If you do, make sure you destroy me the first time, because if you don't, I will die trying to destroy you." He glared for a few seconds, appearing to be shocked that I had said that, and then he slowly turned and walked away.

I was left in utter shock. I was not prone to violence and surely never wanted to do physical harm to anyone. My parents had taught me better, but he stirred feelings in me I could not hold back and the words just came spilling out of my mouth.

That was a sad day for me, because two people who had been such close friends and had enjoyed each other through a common interest were now being separated from each other because of a need to survive within the system. It was unbelievable that two friends could be transformed so quickly—in less than an hour—into potentially bitter enemies solely because of skin color. I was having conflicted feelings because I really liked Lukee and I believed he walked away feeling the same way about me. But the die had been cast and from that day forward we would walk different roads. Instead of being two boys, two friends, we were now two opposites. Lukee and I never exchanged another comic book and never again interacted with each other in a positive way.

After that day, Lukee and I seldom crossed paths. On occasion when we did see each other he always made sure to go in a different direction in order to avoid meeting me face to face. I really felt sorry for Lukee because he was more a victim of his world than I would ever be in my world. In a sense I felt more like the free person and that he was more like the oppressed person. He could not make his own choices but had to abide by the choices his father made for him, and his father was controlled by forces over him. I could decide if I liked him, or if I wanted to treat him with respect. He could not make such a choice. He was learning to hate me, and I always felt that took so much more energy and effort. I, on the other hand, could concentrate on how to help myself rise, while he worked to try keep me down. He wanted ultimately to destroy me, and in the end he would destroy himself. Whenever I return to Lithonia, I often wonder what happened to Lukee.

My family, like most blacks in Lithonia, believed in "root doctors" and fortune tellers. I remember my parents and grandparents driving many miles to see different fortune tellers, hoping to be blessed with good luck. Most of the fortune tellers were white gypsies and wore the prefix "Madam," while most of the root doctors were black and bore such titles as "Doctor Buzzard." Like most black families, mine always worried about not having enough money. Most of the prayers asked God to send good fortune. There was always the search for a symbol of hope, even when it was obviously unreal.

My father was finally cured of such thinking in the early fifties, when he barely escaped with his life—and a television set. It all started when a cousin told him about a gypsy fortune teller who had an outstanding record of predicting the future and telling people how to find their fortune. She lived near Conyers, which was about six miles east of Lithonia, in a trailer with her husband. My father decided to pay a visit. She was set up with a crystal ball and tarot cards. After finishing her initial ritual, she told my father that she could see forty-eight thousand dollars buried somewhere near his house. She convinced him that she could see the money, but she said, "I cannot see the precise location. In order to precisely pinpoint the location of the money, you need a television set." When he questioned why her crystal ball could not pinpoint the location, she responded that it was not strong enough to penetrate rock. She convinced him that only a television set could produce a clear enough picture. My father was convinced she had special powers when she told him that he would have to pass by a big rock before he arrived home. This was true. My dad came home excited and convinced my mother that it was worth taking a chance. The two of them went to the local furniture store, opened a charge account, and purchased a television set for almost six hundred dollars. My father took the television to the gypsy, expecting immediate results. Because an outside antenna was required to produce a clear picture, when she turned on the set only static appeared. She then instructed my father he would need to bring an antenna the next day, at which time she would be able to see the exact location where the money was buried.

That night, as my father lay in bed unable to sleep, he began thinking about what he had been told. It then dawned on him that he had been tricked. In the middle of the night, he got out of bed and told my mother he was going to get his television set. Against my mother's pleas, he went to the trailer and demanded the television set. At first the woman threatened to call the police because she considered the television a gift for her work. We did not know until later that my father had taken his shotgun with him. Apparently, he pulled it out of his car and threatened to start shooting if she didn't give up his television. Upon seeing the gun, the fortune teller and her husband brought the television set out and loaded it in my father's car. He brought the television set home, and that's how we got our first television. My dad obviously never found the forty-eight thousand dollars and he never again visited root doctors or fortune tellers. We became the first family on our street to own a television set. Whenever someone asked us kids how we got our television set, we would say, "A fortune teller got it for us." My dad was not amused.

One day my impetuous nature could have gotten me killed. I had no intention other than to use the restroom at the Lithonia bus station, which had the only public restroom facility for blacks in the downtown area. The sign for the bathroom for "Coloreds" was misspelled "Colred." I had noticed it before, but on this day it irritated me more than normal. I went into the "colored" facility and found it as dirty as usual. There were old tires, oil cans, used batteries, and all other kinds of junk stored in the room. The one nasty commode, which was to be used by both men and women, was dirty and grease-stained. Not only was there no privacy, it was just disgusting.

I did relieve myself and left the room, but as I walked near the white men's bathroom I decided to check it out. I entered and was amazed at how clean it was. I must admit I was impressed. Not only was it clean, it had a urinal and a commode, a nice clean sink, and hand towels. Since there was no place to wash my hands in the other bathroom, I decided to wash them here, which I did. Upon leaving the white men's bathroom, I wondered what the white women's room was like. Since the door was open, I could see it was not occupied, so I went inside. I was only in there for a few seconds, took a brief look around, and was leaving when the biggest white man I had ever seen met me at the door. Someone had seen me go in and decided that I had crossed the line. I knew I was in trouble when this giant of a man said, "What the hell you doing in here, nigger?" Before I could say anything, he grabbed me by the collar and threw me out the door. As I landed on the concrete, I slid across the ground, rubbing the skin off my right forearm. But quickly I realized there was no time for hurting or thinking. Before I could get up I was suddenly jerked to my feet and thrown into the air. As I fell, another fellow kicked at me but missed my head. I began rolling, trying to get up, and as I did, I glimpsed a fellow ready to descend on me with a clenched fist. I rolled again and was finally able to get to my feet. That was the advantage I needed because I knew I could outrun almost anybody. I ran toward home with three burly white men in hot pursuit, all known Klansmen. Lithonia was so small that you pretty well knew who was and who wasn't.

As I ran, I heard one of the men say, "Get the car." I knew I couldn't outrun a car, so as a defensive move I cut across the railroad tracks and headed for some thick woods. When I hit the woods, I began weaving my way through the thicket and began to sense that I was getting some distance between us. Eventually, I heard one say, "To hell with him. I think we taught him a lesson. Let 'im go." I also heard one ask, "Did anybody recognize him?" Another yelled, "I'll know him if I see him again!" Even so, I kept running as hard as I could until I was sure it was safe to stop. I was not too far from home. But I was exhausted, hurting, and scared. I dropped down under a big oak tree. I was starting to hurt all over. But it was more than physical hurt. My pride was hurt, my heart was hurt, and my soul was hurt. I felt helpless and stupid.

My parents and grandparents had tried to warn me about crossing the invisible line, but I had not listened. Now I understood that this line was real and if I strayed too far from the expected norm there would be dire consequences and a high price to pay. I realized that what I had done was purely and simply stupid. My grandfather's words came into my mind again, "Be proud and smart, but don't be stupid." I had not been hurt and could have died, or been seriously injured, because of my stupidity and stubbornness.

Until that fateful day, I had dreamed of the day when I could leave the South and relocate to the North. But this experience completely changed my mind and also taught me a lesson about how fragile my existence could be. I made two promises to myself. The first was never to try to take the system head-on but rather to learn how to maneuver and use it to achieve my goals. The second was that no matter what, I would never leave the South. I decided I had as much right to live, thrive, and enjoy the South as any other person and that I would spend the rest of my life trying to make things better here. From that day forward, I always weighed the risk against the importance of the outcome. My entire life, except for two years in the military, has been wedded to the South.

My mother had an incessant drive to get an education and had completed high school by taking correspondence courses. Of course, growing up in a family environment where most were uneducated, she was looked upon as being weird and others often made fun of her. Family members called her "sensible," but I remember her taking it in stride and plowing ahead towards her goals. She often told me, "Son, there will always be people who will find fault with what you do. Don't let it bother you; just keep on doing what you think is right." She set a wonderful example for me.

My father, in spite of criticism by relatives who believed education was a waste of time and boys should go to work helping support the family, stood firmly in support of my mother's educational pursuits. He made it plain that he expected his children to become educated and achieve more than he had and that he would do everything possible to make it happen. In spite of his limited education, my father was highly intelligent.

My one shining moment in those years came in the tenth grade, when all the years of practicing and performing were put to the test at a high school oratorical contest. It was a night in April 1951, and I was standing alone on a stage at nearby Avondale Colored High School to recite "The Creation," a powerful poem by James Weldon Johnson. That night catapulted me to a new status, and I immediately went from a gawky teenager to a confident public speaker.

Johnson also wrote the gospel hymn "Lift Every Voice." "The Creation" is all about God creating the earth and man. I had never heard anyone recite it, but somehow I let the power of the words take me over. Thankfully, my postpuberty voice had emerged as a smooth baritone with a deep lower register. I can still see and hear myself in triumph on that stage in front of an audience of mostly rowdy, loud, restless teenagers, who up until this point had shown no interest in listening to the speakers.

But when I boomed the first line, "And God stepped out on space," a hush fell over the auditorium, and I felt like I was God himself speaking. I continued,

> And he looked around and said:
> I'm lonely—
> I'll make me a world.

I recited the ten more stanzas that followed, telling the story of God making the sun, the moon, the seven seas, fish, fowl, beasts, and birds, and then I came to the last few lines:

This great God,
Like a mammy bending over her baby,
Kneeled down in the dust,
Toiling over a lump of clay
Till he shaped it in his own image;
Then into it he blew the breath of life,
And Man became a living soul.

At these closing lines, I dropped to my knees, raised my eyes to the heavens, folded my hands in prayer, and boomed out the last words, "Amen, amen."

There was a brief silence, and then the audience burst into applause, rewarding me with my first ever standing ovation. I left the stage, but the applause called me back three times. I won first place. That night my life was changed forever. I knew without a doubt that I wanted to be a public speaker. I owed much of this transition to an outstanding teacher, Mrs. Myrtha Williams.

While still in high school and at age sixteen, I learned a hard lesson about negotiations and contractual agreements. My parents gave me per-

First-ever football team at Bruce Street High School, Lithonia, Georgia. Lee in street shoes without helmet.

mission to take a summer job with a grocer as a delivery boy. In addition to deliveries, I would be required to bag coal, chip ice, and, on each Thursday evening, kill and clean up to sixty chickens. My weekly pay was nine dollars.

I soon found out that all the delivery bicycles were broken and that I would have to walk carrying two or three large bags of groceries. This was boring and tiring, especially on hot days. During many of these long walks, I would let my imagination wander. I would create speeches and pretend I was before a large audience delivering them. After two weeks making an average twelve to fifteen deliveries a day, I decided I needed some form of transportation.

I approached the owner and suggested I could be much more efficient delivering groceries if I had a bicycle. He agreed and sent me to the local bike shop to make a selection. I chose a bike, equipped with a large carry basket, and returned to the store. He expressed delight and then presented me with a document to sign. Instead of providing me with a bike to make deliveries, he expected to deduct five dollars a week from my nine-dollar-a-week paycheck until the bike was paid off. I was shocked and indicated that didn't seem fair, to which he replied, "Life is not fair." I indicated that I didn't like the arrangement and wanted to return the bike. It turned out that was not possible. He indicated that whether I used the bike or whether I continued to work for him, I would have to pay the balance on the bike. It was clear to me, at this young age, I was stuck and had no choice. I agreed and worked the rest of the summer receiving four dollars a week for six twelve-hour days working at the grocery store.

As everywhere else across the South, there were two separate but unequal school systems in Lithonia. Lithonia had just two high schools: Lithonia High, for whites, and Lithonia Colored High, for blacks. The schools were located on opposite sides of town. The white school received the new books and equipment, while the black school received the white school hand-me-downs. During my entire twelve years, I never had a new textbook or sat at a new desk. The white school had a state-of-the-art gymnasium, while the black school had no gym. There were approximately three hundred students in all grades at the black school and approximately the same at the white school.

The tenth grade was a banner year of progress at Lithonia Colored High School. The first school band was formed, under the direction of our first band director. The band consisted of twenty-eight instruments, which were purchased with proceeds from community fundraisers. I played trumpet along with my sister Louise and my brother Walter. We also got our first football/basketball coach. I was optimistic that we might finally have a winning sports program, especially a basketball team.

We had a basketball team mostly in name only. All of our games were played in our street shoes outside on a dirt court. Our uniforms were handed down from the white school and from area colleges such as Georgia Tech. We had two basketballs, one for practice and one for games. I enjoyed playing basketball but didn't care much about football. I went on the football field one time, was hit in the face, and never went back again. At six feet I was one of the tallest players on the basketball team, and I thought, with good coaching, I could be good enough to play in college. That never happened; consequently, I never played in college.

There was one encouraging time when our coach received permission from the white high school principal and coach to allow us to practice in the white gym for a big upcoming game with Conyers. The request was made because inclement weather had prevented us from practicing outside. We were astounded when the request was granted. We concluded that since the white principal at Lithonia High School was both new and from the North he didn't know he was violating custom. On the other hand, we knew the coach was local and were shocked when he agreed. We arrived at the gym after the white players had left. Needless to say we were a little nervous but very excited to be inside a real gym. We changed into our faded and bedraggled uniforms in the locker room and took to the court. We had been practicing about a half an hour when suddenly the doors burst open and there stood a group of angry-looking white men. We recognized most of them as Klansmen. What was most shocking, however, was that heading the group was "Mr. Charlie" Davidson, the chairman of the county school board of education. He wasn't a Klansman, but a sympathizing manipulator, as were most upper-class whites.

He yelled, "Who the hell is in charge of you niggers?" The coach, obviously very nervous, responded, "I am, Mr. Davidson." Davidson then asked, "What the hell you doing in this gymnasium?" Coach said that he had asked the principal and coach if he could hold a practice there after the white team finished. Davidson then said, "Y'all stay right here and don't you move. I'm going and get them boys over here."

After about thirty minutes, Davidson returned with the principal. In the center of the gym, he asked him in a very loud voice, pointing to our coach, "Did you give this 'boy' permission to bring these nigger kids in this gym?" Davidson must have expected the principal to deny giving permission, which would have then given him an excuse to let the Klan thugs attack us. I actually expected the white principal to take the easy way out and deny it. Amazingly, he looked Davidson in the eye and said, "Yes, I did. I don't see any harm in letting these kids use this gym when it is standing idle. Since they don't have a gym and we do, why not let them use it from time to time?" We were shocked because we had never witnessed a white man standing in defense of any blacks, especially against "Mr. Charlie." We were convinced that he did not understand where he was and certainly didn't understand that if there was anything worse than being a "nigger" in Georgia, it was being a "nigger lover." I was wise enough to know that he was digging a deep hole for himself. But he showed no signs of backing down. Davidson had turned blood red and was so angry that he started to shake. He retorted, "You, you mean, you let these niggers come in here and contaminate our gym? You mean you had the gall to create this kind of problem? I guess next you're going to want to let them in classrooms. Who gives you the authority to make such a decision?"

The principal remained very calm and showed no signs of nervousness as Davidson continued to rant and rave. Within a few minutes, which felt more like hours, he calmed down and said to our coach, "OK, I guess this ain't your fault this time. So we gonna let you go, but if you are ever caught anywhere near this school in the future, we will not have any mercy, do you understand?" Coach responded, "Yes, sir." With that he motioned us to leave. We were all so glad that we headed for the cars as fast as we could run, leaving all our street clothes in the locker room.

The next day a local police officer returned our clothes to our school. He also informed our principal that the white principal had been fired and was to be out of town "before the sun sets today." He went on to gleefully proclaim, "That's what we do for nigger lovers around here." We never heard from that principal again, although we learned much later that he had gotten a job in an Atlanta school. Amazingly, the white coach never did show up that night and was also fired by "Mr. Charlie" the next day. However, with his connections, within three days, he was reinstated as coach by a majority vote of the county school board. Our coach never talked about practicing in the gym again and we kept on losing games. We lost our game to Conyers, as we expected, and did not win a game that year. That year, as had been the case the year before, we played Tallapoosa in the tournament, the second-worst team in the county. Our team was so bad even Tallapoosa beat us mercilessly for its only victory of the year. What was even worse is that every other school had matching uniforms, which made us both the worst team and the worst-looking team in the tournament.

A few months after the white gym fiasco, we were shocked again, when the principal at Lithonia Colored High School summoned our coach to his office to hand over six new basketballs that had just been delivered. Both the coach and the principal wondered why the balls were there, since neither of them had placed such an order. They finally concluded that this must be a peace offering for the incident at the gym earlier. We had never had more than two basketballs at once, so we were elated that we had six new ones.

Later that day we were playing with several of the new balls, when the principal and the postman came to take them from us. The principal explained that the postman, who should have known better, had delivered the balls to the wrong school. They were supposed to go to Lithonia High School, not Lithonia Colored High School. All six balls were taken, washed, repackaged, and delivered to the white high school. But when their coach discovered that black kids had been playing with the balls, he refused to accept them. The angry and embarrassed postman was forced to bring them back to us. During the remainder of my time there, our school never got another new ball.

The following week the school board called an emergency meeting and voted unanimously to change the name of our school to Bruce Street High School. There was no public notice, no outcry, and no public input. It was just done to avoid future delivery mix-ups. It felt strange that I would end the eleventh grade at Lithonia Colored High but enter the twelfth grade and graduate from Bruce Street High. There was a side benefit for the seven of us who comprised the senior class. We were delighted that we would not have the word "colored" on our diploma.

I had actually considered dropping out of school at the end of the tenth grade. In spite of my mother's encouragement, I was struggling to see what difference an education would make in my life. I had the best-paying job I had ever had, driving a truck for a lumber and building supply company. My parents were struggling financially, and I felt I needed to help lighten the load. At least, that's how I explained it to my mother when she challenged my decision. I finally calmed her by promising that I would work only a few weeks after school started and would then enroll. She accepted that, but I was sure I would not return to school. Things were going great. I was making a lot of overtime and consequently earning greater amounts of money.

Best All Round Student in the 1953 graduating class, Bruce Street High School.

Then fate intervened. It was a rainy day and there was nothing to do. I was sitting in the warehouse reading a book when the owner came in and spotted me. He asked why I was sitting around and not working. I responded that I had completed all that I saw needed doing. He then said, "Well, I got something for you to do." Being a willing worker, I followed him to the main store, where he pointed to the bathroom. He directed me to clean it. When I finished, he came in and spotted some feces in the commode and directed that I use steel wool to clean them off. I asked for some rubber gloves, to which he replied, "Just use your bare hands, it won't poison you." I considered this to be over the line and refused to do it. He then said, "Either do it or go find another job." He was shocked when I told him that he had done what my mother had failed to do. I said, "You just confirmed why I need to go back to school and get an education." I walked out and went directly to the school, met with the assistant principal, Mr. C. C. Howell, and enrolled for my eleventh-grade year.

Later in the week, while in conversation with Mrs. Williams, my English and speech teacher, I confided that I was still having trouble determining what good an education would be without opportunity. Mrs. Williams held my hand and looked me directly in the eyes and said, "Nat, I cannot promise you that you will ever have an opportunity, but I can guarantee that if an opportunity should ever come to you, you will be ready and prepared to seize it." (Everybody called me Nat to avoid confusion with my father, whose name was also Howard.) She reminded me how I had won the oratorical contest because I was ready and prepared. "That," she said, "was an unexpected opportunity that you seized successfully, because you were prepared." Mr. Howell suggested that I quit the basketball team and concentrate on improving my grade point average during my last year of high school in order to increase my chances of being accepted by a college. At the end of the eleventh grade, I made straight As and was second in my class. I was very optimistic that I could be named valedictorian, a thought that had never before crossed my mind.

Early during my senior year, I applied for admission to Ohio State University because my maternal grandfather lived in Columbus. However, Mrs. Williams and Mr. Howell strongly suggested that I apply to Clark, a small private college in Atlanta. My parents were concerned about the high tuition but were assured that if I were accepted, there could be enough scholarship funding to cover tuition.

I worked hard that entire year but, unfortunately, lost the valedictorian slot to a young lady in my class. I came in second. But all was not lost. I had been accepted to Clark and had been awarded more than enough scholarship money to cover tuition. I was most excited about having been chosen by the faculty to receive an award from the *Atlanta Journal* as the Best All Round Student. As it turned out, this was even better than being valedictorian.

I learned later this decision did not come without its price. The principal, Mr. Flagg, did not think I deserved the honor and tried to veto the faculty choice. But Mr. Howell and Mrs. Williams refused to give in, and the faculty voted unanimously against the principal. At the graduation ceremony, the principal refused to present me the silver cup, which was presented instead by Mr. Howell. That cup has never been out of my possession, except when I was in the military.

Mr. Charlie Davidson, as the lifetime chairman of the school board, delivered the commencement address in spite of the senior class protest. I have never forgotten the feelings I had listening to him insult and berate the faculty and all "niggers." Davidson referred to our principal as "Flagg," never using his initials of C. E., or his title. He said that "Flagg" understood how to stay in his place and that more of our "nigger" teachers needed to learn that. He recounted the gymnasium incident, informing us that we would never be equal to whites. He said that we were the underclass and that whites were the superior class. He said he wanted us to know how lucky we were to be getting an education and that we needed to learn how to show more appreciation to white folks for letting us have this privilege.

I had never before nor have I since listened to a speech more intently than I did that night. As I sat there, I began building a resistance to everything he was preaching. I was determined not to be restricted to "my place." I was not inferior to anybody, white or black. I was not going to be humble and scrape and bow as Mr. Flagg did that night and many times before and after. By the time he finished, Davidson had created a determination inside of a young boy to try to be the best and always strive toward equality. I knew we were being educated in an inferior school, but I believed that in spite of the school, I could learn enough to compete with students from better schools. After that night, I was ready for the next step.

A few months later, when I arrived on the campus of Clark College in Atlanta, I learned that I may have been ready for the next step but was far from being ready for college. It didn't take long for me to realize that in spite of good teaching, the lack of adequate resources at my high school meant that college courses would be a real challenge. I quickly understood this would be a huge horse to mount and ride. Ready, I jumped on and held tight.

Plate 1. Lee inducted into the Education Hall of Fame at East Carolina University, Greenville, North Carolina.

Plate 2. The Lee family: the last family picture before the death of grandson Nicholas (eyes closed). (Back row, Left to Right) Ricky, Janet, Nicholas, Lillian, Howard, Angela, and Karin; (front row) Jillian (center) and Jaimie.

Plate 3. Lee's maternal grandfather, Charlie Vaughn (formerly Barnes); he lived and died in Columbus, Ohio.

Plate 4. Lee's mother and father, Howard and Lou Tempie Lee.

Plate 5. One of the seven concessions stores owned by Lee at the Raleigh-Durham International Airport.

Plate 6. Lee's father, Howard Lee, speaking at a fundraising event for the campaign for lieutenant governor, 1976.

Plate 7. Lillian Lee and Howard N. Lee.

Plate 8. Grandchildren Jaimie, Jillian, and Nicholas. This is the last picture taken of Nicholas before his death at age fifteen.

Plate 9. The house the Lees purchased at 504 Tinkerbell Road, making them the first family to integrate a neighborhood in Chapel Hill.

Plate 10. Canoeing on the French Broad River, western North Carolina. This was Lee's first time in a canoe.

Plate 11. Lillian confers with Terry Sanford at a dinner honoring Lee's service to North Carolina.

Plate 12. *Escorting Hugh Boyd to the polls to vote in 1972 U.S. congressional campaign in the second district. Boyd's first vote was cast in 1896 for George White, the last black congressman from the South until the 1970s.*

Plate 13. The swearing-in ceremony for the North Carolina Senate. Facing the camera to Lee's left is Senator Russell Walker.

Plate 14. With Terry Sanford, attending a Bill Clinton for President rally in Hillsborough, North Carolina.

Plate 15. Visit with Mrs. Lady Bird Johnson. Left to right: Lillian Lee, Governor Jim Hunt, Howard Lee, Lady Bird Johnson.

Plate 16. Escorting Governor Jim Hunt on an inspection tour of the North Carolina Zoological Park. On the right, in a blue jacket, is zoo director Robert Frye.

Plate 17. Lee and Governor Jim Hunt in serious discussion.

Plate 18. Howard N. Lee, secretary of the Department of Natural Resources.

Plate 19. Howard Lee conversing with long-time advisor Walter R. Davis.

Plate 20. The Lee siblings: (front row, Left to Right) Howard, Minnard, Walter, and Louise Lee Hall. Standing in the back (Left to Right) are Larry Lee, Mary Lee, Annie Lois McCaskill, and Frankie Lee.

Plate 21. With Governor Michael Easley, wife Lillian, and daughter Angela at the swearing-in ceremony for Lee's appointment to the North Carolina Utilities Commission.

Plate 22. Pictured with (Left to Right) Judge Carl Fox, who administered the oath, daughter Angela, godson David Elliott, and wife Lillian.

Plate 23. Lunch with elementary schoolchildren, Charlotte.

6 College Years

"**Y**ou have come from places from all across this nation to attend one of the most prestigious black schools in the South. This is Clark College, founded in 1869 to provide higher education for freed slaves, and today, an elite institution of higher learning. You have come from places where you were big fish in little ponds, but now you are at Clark College, where you are a little fish in a big pond. Here, my young friends, you will learn to swim well and learn to swim quickly or you will sink fast. I challenge you to apply yourselves and focus all your attention on learning how to be a good swimmer or you won't survive." These words were spoken by one of the college deans to my freshman class. I was really scared, but at the same time I was so proud to be the first ever in the history of my family to enroll in college. I was also confident that I was ready and could compete. I had graduated as salutatorian of my class at Bruce Street. There were only seven of us in the class, but it still felt like an achievement.

I was somewhat disappointed that I couldn't live on campus. My mother and father just could not afford to pay the dormitory rent. They arranged to rent a room in the home of my father's maternal aunt, who lived approximately four miles from campus. They agreed to pay her one hundred dollars a month for a room and breakfast. I would occupy the room from Sunday night through Thursday night, spending weekends at home. I would return from campus late at night to a freezing cold room. My breakfast was the worst ever—two slices of burned toast and a bowl of cold vegetable soup. My entire time in the house this never changed. Eventually, I simply refused to eat the food and many times attended class hungry. This arrangement lasted for only one semester and made my life a living hell.

When I finally shared this with my parents, they became very angry, and after that first semester we decided that during the next one I should stay at home in Lithonia and travel the eighteen miles to campus by bus each day. I would leave home at 5 A.M., arriving at campus in time for my 8

Lee as a freshman in college.

o'clock class. I would generally leave campus most evenings around 6 P.M. and arrive home at 8 P.M. Occasionally, one of my friends would allow me to sleep in a chair in his dormitory room.

My first year in college was a real challenge, financially, academically, and physically. I made my life even more challenging by choosing a pre-med major. My first-semester course schedule was one of the toughest in my class, and at the end of the semester my grades were a disaster. I had registered to take chemistry, algebra, and biology. From the very first day I was lost and realized how woefully unprepared I was for college. Yet I convinced myself that if I studied hard enough, I could overcome my weaknesses and succeed. I studied hard, received a lot of help from professors, and was supported and encouraged by classmates, but in the end that wasn't enough. I received Fs in all of my math and science courses, but managed to pass my English and religion courses. The second semester, I enrolled in liberal arts classes, hoping to raise my grade point average. I did quite well and received above-average grades. Being convinced my living arrangement had contributed to my lack of success, I was determined that during my second year I would arrange to stay on campus. However,

I knew I would need to earn a lot more money during the summer, as well as continue to work on campus during the school year.

A friend and classmate, Carl Fanning, suggested we should spend the summer working in New York, where we could make a lot more money. It was not easy, but my parents reluctantly agreed to support my decision. We spent one week in New York and had no success getting a job. I was ready to return home, but we decided to try our luck in Atlantic City before throwing in the towel. We had very little money left and spent three days job hunting, with no success. We had so little money we were eating canned pork and beans and white bread twice a day. After a week in New York and now three days in Atlantic City with no job, I decided it was time to go home. The last day, and the last can of pork and beans, we got a call from the Traymore Hotel offering us jobs. Carl was hired as the chief short-order cook and I as a bus boy. The pay was much more than I would have made working in Georgia.

I learned a lot about myself and concluded that my teenage decision to stay in the South was the right one. While I grew up believing that life for blacks in the North was better, I quickly learned that was not true. I found that blacks lived in segregated sections of town and performed many low-paying jobs, mostly as workers, not supervisors. While I enjoyed my experience in Atlantic City, I preferred my life in the South. I earned enough money during that summer to pay my tuition and dormitory rent. However, I did continue to work part-time every weekend in the dining hall at college and at the Biltmore Hotel in Atlanta, as a waiter and bartender.

In spite of having to work weekends, I was still convinced that I had the ability to pass the same three courses I had failed the first year. One faculty advisor suggested that I was a glutton for punishment and should switch majors and take different courses. I felt that would be admitting defeat, so instead I decided to enroll in the same courses again, determined that I would pass this time. I spent every free hour studying, but in the end it was like the rerun of a bad movie. I failed the same three courses.

After the second fiasco, I finally got the message—I was not going to be a doctor and needed to chart a new direction for my life. I was feeling beaten down. Throughout my life I had believed I could overcome any obstacle, but now self-doubt was starting to cloud my optimism. I questioned whether I should accept defeat and settle for being a college dropout. Of the three Bruce Street High graduates in my class who had enrolled in college, I was the only one left. I had hoped to be the first at the school to graduate from college.

Lee as chief short-order cook, Traymore Hotel, Atlantic City, New Jersey, 1958.

As usual, I mentioned my feelings to my mother. She had overcome many barriers in her life. She insisted that I refuse to quit and told me that I should never use the word "defeat." At the conclusion of our talk, I felt more optimistic, but I was still feeling doubtful. She handed me a book of motivational quotes and pointed to the one that made a complete shift in my attitude. It read, "I'm a little wounded but I am not slain, I shall lay me down for to bleed a while, then I'll rise and fight with you again." As I read those words (by the English poet John Dryden, and often quoted by the entrepreneur Jack Kent Cooke), I could feel a surge of determination returning. I wrote those words on a piece of paper and stuck the paper in my wallet. Any time I felt doubt creeping into my mind, I would retrieve it and read the words.

I decided that I should change my major to sociology and consider shifting my career path towards law. During the second semester of my sophomore year at Clark, my grades improved, but they were still subpar in comparison to my classmates. My highest grade was an A in logic. I made Cs in sociology and anthropology and a B in history. I switched my minor to religion and took a course on the Bible. My grades were acceptable, but not high enough to lift my grade point average above the red zone.

In 1955 I applied to summer school because I knew I was on the verge of being kicked out unless my grade point average was raised. Unfortunately, and to my surprise, I was not allowed to enroll for summer school because my grades were too low. I was confused. If my grades were too low for summer school how could I qualify for a third year? When I was invited to enroll for my third year, I was really surprised.

I managed to complete my third year at Clark with a C average. Even though I was on probation, I felt like my grades were good enough for me to be admitted for my fourth year. I returned to Atlantic City during the summer of 1956, but not as a bus boy. I was hired as the chief short-order cook. This time I was much better prepared. I missed having grits for breakfast, so I took enough grits to last through the summer. Some guests, however, learned about my cooking grits and began requesting grits as a part of their breakfast order. Eventually, the hotel decided to add grits to the menu, and it became one of the more popular items. In July 1956 I received a letter saying that I would not be welcomed back at Clark for a fourth year. I was working at the Traymore Hotel in Atlantic City when I got the letter. I immediately quit and boarded a Greyhound bus to Lithonia. After riding all night, I arrived early on the morning of July 10. I was aware that either I had to be enrolled in college or I would be drafted into the U.S. Army—and I much preferred the college option.

My mother thought I might be accepted at Fort Valley State, a small black college near Macon. Although my mother had been a student there, I didn't have a very high opinion of the college. But I finally decided that Fort Valley was my one and only shot of getting into another college. At 10 o'clock on the night of July 11, I boarded another Greyhound bus and went to Fort Valley. I arrived on campus at 9 o'clock in the morning and went directly to the office of the registrar. Even though I did not have an appointment, the registrar agreed to see me. I told him my story and pleaded for a chance to enroll. He said he didn't have that authority but that he would take me to see the president, Mr. C. V. Troup. I was amazed that the president would even see me. President Troup was a well-dressed, slender man in his forties, with thick, wavy hair. He spent more than twenty minutes with me as I told him of my hopes and dreams for life. Then he said, "For whatever reason, I like you and I am willing to take a chance on you. We'll need to see your high school and college transcripts. Regardless of what we find, I am authorizing that you be admitted on probation for one quarter. If you make one grade less than a C, you're out. We have no scholarship funds; therefore, you'll have to pay your own tuition. We have no housing allowance, so you'll have to pay to live in the dorm." I immediately said, "I'll take it." I had no idea where I would get the money, but somehow I just believed things would work out.

I left the campus elated. I spent the night in the Macon bus station and arrived back in Lithonia in the late afternoon. I had already called and shared the good news with my mother and had asked her to think about how we could raise the money. Fort Valley was a financial bargain compared to Clark. My parents had already decided that they would go to the Household Finance Company. They borrowed the money, using some furniture and the car as collateral. I promised them I would get a job in the college dining hall, but my mother said no. She wanted me to concentrate on succeeding because, as she put it, "This may be your last chance."

I decided to keep sociology as my major and took several related courses. The president took a personal interest in me. He kept up with my grades, and any time he saw me goofing off he would tell me I had better get to work. I joined the chorus, and the choir director took a very direct interest in me as well. He encouraged me to take voice lessons, which I did.

Dr. Troup (he received his Ph.D. after my first year) was a strong Phi Beta Sigma fraternity man. Amazingly, while at Clark I had viewed the Phi Beta Sigma fraternity as a joke because it was considered to be the fraternity of nerds because these were not the boys who were sought after by the girls. These were the boys who spent time studying and who were the wallflowers at dances.

In spite of this image, I had decided that I would join the fraternity because of the president's affiliation. After all, I had determined that with the support of the president a lot of doors could be easily opened. My second year in the fraternity and my senior year I was elected president. I was committed to transforming Phi Beta Sigma into the fraternity of envy on the campus. I challenged the members to adopt a community support mission and engage in community service. In the end, the brothers joined forces to bring Christmas to needy kids in Fort Valley. We went out and collected used toys. Then, between September and December, we refurbished bicycles and all kinds of toys. Just before we went home for the Christmas holiday break, we invited selected kids to campus to choose a toy for

Graduation picture, 1959. Fort Valley State College, Georgia. Photograph courtesy of Maddox Studio, Fort Valley, Georgia.

Christmas. This was a tremendous hit. Before I left campus I convinced the other fraternities and sororities to join us in a unified effort. I was very proud when I checked back the following Christmas and was told they had assembled and distributed hundreds of toys to local kids.

I thoroughly enjoyed college life at Fort Valley and made one B and all Cs the first quarter. After that my mother relented and allowed me to work in the dining hall. I ended my first year at Fort Valley on the honor roll and maintained the position until I graduated with honors.

During my three years at Fort Valley, Dr. C. V. Troup became my primary mentor. He was a visionary, stern man who had a velvet touch. He set a high standard and expected the students to excel. He especially focused on me because, as he would tell me later, he felt I was an untapped gold mine of talent. In addition to performing with the chorus, I joined the playmakers' theater at his insistence and engaged in public speaking. I was chosen to be the radio sportscaster for the college.

When I graduated from Fort Valley State in 1959 after three years, I became the first person in my family and the first person from Bruce Street High School to graduate from college. My mother received her degree in elementary education from Fort Valley in August 1959 and became the second person in our family to earn a college degree.

7 Surviving the Army

had graduated from college planning to enroll in law school because I felt it was probably the only profession where I could have some control over my destiny. The usual choices at that time for blacks were to teach, preach, or go work in the post office. I didn't want to do any of those. I applied to the University of Georgia Law School, but before I was accepted, I received the dreaded letter ordering me to report for active duty. On August 8, 1959, I reported to the U.S. Army Processing Depot in Atlanta to begin serving two years of active duty. I was not surprised to receive this draft order because I had been given six deferments in order to complete my undergraduate degree.

I had hated the thought of going into the army because I felt it was taking time out of my life that I didn't want to sacrifice. I was, also, basically unhappy with how black soldiers were being treated in America. Black soldiers had fought in World War II and returned home to the same segregation and repression they had left. I felt I would experience the same treatment as those brave soldiers who had fought to protect the freedom they never enjoyed. I was angry that I couldn't see any hope that things would change.

I reported as directed to the center in Atlanta but hoped I would not be processed. My hope of being released from the draft was enhanced because I watched several white draftees given release papers for a variety of reasons. For example, a former football player from Clemson University, who had been drafted by the Chicago Bears football team, was released when his congressman intervened. He was instead assigned to a reserve unit. This gave me an idea, and I asked myself, why not call my congressman and ask if he would intervene for me? I placed a call to the staff person in his Atlanta office and was told there was little they could do, but they would try. A call was made from his office to the Pentagon, which directed the processing center to hold me until further notice. Consequently, my draft class was shipped out without me. I was held at the processing center for three days. On the third day I was informed that my request had been denied and I would be shipped out later that day on a bus leaving for Fort Jackson, South Carolina.

It was late afternoon when the bus entered the gates at Fort Jackson. I realized I was about to experience an environment like none I had ever known. I felt as if I was on the verge of stepping into a huge body of water and (just as I had been warned at Clark College) would either learn to swim quickly and survive or sink fast and perish.

We were greeted by a short, stocky, black sergeant, who looked like one big muscle. His arms appeared to be the size of my legs and his chest looked like a block wall. He stood erect, watching as his staff directed us to line up side by side. I thought this might not be so bad; after all, the man in charge was a "brother." This assumption was a colossal mistake. A few minutes later I knew there would be no favoritism from this guy. He forcefully made it clear that during the next eight weeks we could give "our hearts to God" because "our asses" belonged to him. He emphasized further that we should "keep our eyes open, our mouths shut, and not volunteer for anything." He then asked for six volunteers to walk fireguard that night. I must have had a case of amnesia because I was the first to volunteer. The other guys could not believe I had been that stupid. One guy standing next to me asked, "What's the matter with you, fool?" I was starting to wonder the same thing. Nobody else volunteered. Then the sergeant glared at me for a few seconds, put his face close to mine almost touching noses and asked, "Soldier can't you follow orders? Didn't you listen to me earlier? All you get for your stupidity is to stay up all night guarding the barracks. Step over here soldier and give me five." I was so naive that I walked over to where he was as he said again, "Give me five." I actually thought he meant a high-five, like the style of slapping hands in celebration the way we did it back in Lithonia. I had the audacity to think he wanted to congratulate me for volunteering. He then directed that I get down and do five pushups. After I finished the pushups, he drafted five other soldiers. We were designated fireguards for the night, and issued nightsticks and helmets.

As I walked around the barracks during my shift, I could hear the lucky ones in the barracks snoring. I repeated over and over as I walked, "Keep your eyes open, your mouth shut, and don't volunteer for nothing." By the time the watch was over, those words were solidly burned in my mind. From that day forward I did not always keep my mouth shut, but I did keep my eyes open and never volunteered for a single thing.

The next morning, following breakfast, I was designated one of a group being ordered to Fort Benning, Georgia, for basic training. I was exhausted from pulling fireguard duty but was grateful for the opportunity to spend several relaxing hours on a bus, thinking I could get some much needed sleep. However, I soon found out there was no such thing as down time in the army. We were lectured during the entire trip on military protocol and procedures. I was now convinced my two years in the army would feel like an eternity.

Once at Fort Benning I struggled to adjust to the regimentation. Getting out of bed at 5 A.M. every day was a real chore. Performing the daily exercise routine every morning was a strenuous challenge. I constantly failed the daily and weekly personal inspections. After about two weeks, I accepted I would be in the army for two years and I could either shape up and make the best of the situation or be miserable for two years. From that point forward, I found the experience more tolerable.

Life at Fort Benning exposed me to my first desegregated living experience. All my life I had accepted that whites were smart. However, it didn't take long for me to realize that was far from being true. In class I consistently outscored many of the whites. My parents and grandparents had constantly warned me to never trust a white man. Every night I struggled to adjust to sleeping in the same barracks. Eventually, I began to feel comfortable and focused less on their skin color and more on developing friendly personal relationships.

By the end of six weeks, I was rated among the top 10 sharpest soldiers in my company of about 125. My improvement was so remarkable that I was among five soldiers selected and invited to attend Officer Candidate School. I was excited about the prospect of becoming an officer. But once I found it would require me to extend my tour of duty by an additional three years, I declined the offer.

I completed basic training and received numerous awards. To my surprise, I was assigned to the medical training facility at Fort Sam Houston, Texas, for eight weeks of medical corpsman training. I was pleased and for the first time began to feel excited about being in the army. I arrived at Fort Sam Houston with my most positive attitude and was starting to really enjoy being in the army. I was determined to become a model soldier. I put special emphasis on being "spit and polished" from head to foot. I was always prepared for class. I was also completely unaware that I was being observed by the first sergeant, until he called me into his quarters one evening.

First Sergeant Hot, who was of Asian descent, told me he had been watching me and had become convinced that I had leadership qualities.

He asked if I would accept the role of barracks leader. My duties would be securing the barracks at night and reporting on those who violated curfew. I was to make sure that the barracks were clean and neat at all times and resolve any problems. I was speechless and flattered. I knew this would be the most important leadership role I had ever held and a very big opportunity for me. However, I was a little concerned about how the white soldiers would respond to me. I raised this question with the first sergeant. His response was that I had been selected because it was clear most of the soldiers of all races respected and trusted me. I accepted the assignment. The announcement was made the next morning at roll call. There was mixed reaction. I pledged to be fair and treat everyone with dignity and respect.

I was assigned my own private room. For the first time in my life I did not have to share a room or a bed with anyone. I thoroughly enjoyed the perks that went with the position. I was granted automatic weekend passes, excused from all guard and kitchen duty, and not subjected to weekly inspections. However, as part of my duties I was responsible for conducting inspections in my barracks and making recommendations for weekend passes.

During our time together, I had worked hard and gained the trust of the troops. I was pleased to see the men had developed great pride in the fact that we were rated the best barracks in the company. I established an advisory council, which helped enhance their confidence and keep channels of communication open. We grew to be a close-knit group in spite of being the most diverse barracks in the company. The group consisted of whites, blacks, Latinos, and Asians. Things went extremely well for the first seven of the eight weeks of basic. This had not been the case in some other barracks, where there had been fist fights, disturbances late at night, and even some soldiers being court martialed. I had hoped we would be incident-free through graduation.

Unfortunately, my optimism was dashed one Saturday morning, when a white soldier, John Terry, decided to beat up a Latino soldier, Javier Sanchez. Terry was upset because Sanchez was speaking Spanish and he couldn't understand what he was saying. When I confronted Terry about his behavior, he grew even angrier. He turned to me and walked up very close with his nose almost touching mine. He turned as red as a beet as he yelled, "I'm not here to protect no Spanish Latin-speaking wetbacks, just like I ain't here to protect no niggers like you!" I was shocked because this was the first time I had heard that word since becoming a soldier. I hated that word with very deep passion. At that moment I felt myself growing very angry. But I was able to restrain myself as I heard a voice inside me saying, "Use your mind not your muscle. The mind is mightier than the muscle." I gained control over my own emotions, and then spoke in a calm but authoritative voice directing both soldiers to my quarters.

After extensive discussion, Terry extended his hand and made an apology to the Latino soldier, which Sanchez accepted. Immediately, Terry turned and apologized to me, saying he had not used the "N" word since he left his home state of Mississippi. I accepted his apology but warned him that he would be in deep trouble if he used that word at the wrong time and in the wrong place among black soldiers. I said I would file a report but recommend no action beyond a warning.

Later, as I sat alone in my quarters, there was a knock on my door. It was Terry, asking if he could speak. He wanted to explain how being raised in Mississippi he had been told that "Negroes" were nothing but "trash." He went on to say how much he had resented my being made the barracks leader and confessed that he felt he had deserved the appointment. "I must admit," he said, "that you have been fair and treated us all with respect." He acknowledged harboring a lot of pent-up anger after being denied admission to Officer Candidate School.

After discussing the episode with the first sergeant, we decided there had to be some form of punishment and that I should be the one to decide it. I called both soldiers into my quarters and assigned each one two straight days of extra duties, to include cleaning the bathrooms and cleaning the area of litter and cigarette butts. I announced to the other soldiers what actions were being taken and why. There were no further incidents during my tenure.

On the last scheduled day at camp, we all gathered to receive our orders and our next duty assignment. I had been assured I would be staying at Fort Sam Houston for advance medic training. So I was shocked to learn that instead I was being sent to Fort Hood, Texas, to a heavy artillery company. I spoke with the company clerk, the first sergeant, and the company commander, and all confirmed my orders were correct. The commander summoned me into his office to tell me that the quota for advanced medic training had been filled and I had been cut because I was not Regular Army, just a two-year draftee.

That afternoon, sad and disappointed, I boarded a bus bound for Fort Hood, Texas. The love I had begun to develop for the army had started to wane.

8 A Letter to the President

It was halfway through December 1959 when I arrived at Fort Hood, Texas. I knew that I would be spending Christmas on base. This was not a happy time for me. In addition to being disappointed with my assignment, I was also sad that I would be away from home and family at Christmas for the first time in my life. I did not know it at the time, but I was about to experience a series of events that would change my life forever.

I arrived at Fort Hood with a bad attitude, a big ego, and a chip on my shoulder. I was assigned to the barracks with a group of guys who were old-timers at that post and mostly career soldiers. I was the only draftee and college graduate in the barracks. This was the barracks assigned to the motor pool, whose basic responsibility was repairing and operating tanks. I was immediately designated as a tank driver trainee. Once word got out about my background, I became the target of ridicule and was often referred to as "the brain." Some even joked that I would be the most educated tank driver they had ever had at Fort Hood. One soldier walked up to me and said, "Hell, you went to college and you ain't no better than me in the army and I didn't finish high school." I had no intention of being the "best educated tank driver at Fort Hood" or anywhere else in the army. When I said that, they all broke out laughing. As one soldier said, "What you gonna do about it? All you gonna get is your ass put in the stockade." I knew that was a real possibility. But it was a risk I had to take. I would drive a tank only if I failed to get my assignment changed.

I was careful to observe military protocol, up to a point. I explained my interest to the first sergeant, who granted me permission to speak with the captain. When I arrived at company headquarters, I was seated at a table in the captain's office to wait. While there, in the quiet of the office, I began to think maybe this wasn't such a good idea. I was tempted to leave, but realized that if I didn't complete this journey, I would always regret not having followed through with my plan. The captain arrived and appeared to be a mild-mannered person, but obviously strict military. He

Official army portrait, Fort Hood, Texas.

listened attentively as I explained that as a college graduate, I felt I was being wasted by the army. I mentioned several areas where I thought my contributions would be more valuable, for example as a counselor in the mental health clinic, a specialist in the personnel office, or a legal assistant in the adjutant general's office. He let me finish and then responded, saying, "Private, your best course of action is to accept your assignment, do your job, and work toward getting an honorable discharge when your tour of duty is complete."

I was disappointed in the captain's attitude. I then told him I did not think reassigning me would set a precedent, since I knew several white soldiers had been reassigned after their congressmen had intervened. I cited one without a background in law or a college degree who had been transferred to the adjutant general's office. I said, "Captain, I hope the army will give me the same consideration."

He gave me a stern look, then in a very angry voice warned me that if I made trouble, then I would get trouble. "The last thing I need," he said, "is for somebody to start injecting racial friction on this base. You are ordered to return to your duty station, fall in line, and do your job."

I went back to the tank motor pool dejected and feeling hopeless. I was beginning to think I needed to accept that I was stuck here and should get on with doing the job.

An older black soldier came over, put his hand on my shoulder, and said, "Boy, you just wasting your time. You ain't gonna win this fight. Nobody beats this man's army, and if you keep acting like this, you gonna get washed up, washed out, and dishonorably discharged. Listen to me, son. You a young man, and you got a good life ahead. Two years ain't that long. Do your job. Finish your time and then go do what you want with your life. You keep stirring things up and you gonna mess things up for yourself and maybe even for the rest of us black soldiers."

I listened respectfully and then explained that this was more than just what job I performed, it was a matter of pride and fairness and respect. I told him I had identified many white soldiers who had barely finished high school performing cushy jobs in the personnel office and the budget office. He started to walk away. He then returned and said, "Lee, you gonna make trouble for us, and we don't need trouble. You just here to do two years. This is the only decent way some of us can make a living and I don't want you screwing it up. As a matter of fact, we ain't gonna let you screw it up."

I said to him, "I understand your position and I will do my best not to screw it up for you and for me. But if I don't fight this, if I don't stand up for what I believe in, and if I don't push for equal treatment, things will never change. I may lose in the end, but if I do, I will at least know in my heart I gave it my best shot. If I do that, I will not have to apologize to the next generation for my complacency." I told him that at the induction center in Atlanta most of the people I saw there were whites, sitting at desks and talking on the telephone, performing administrative jobs in air-conditioned offices.

At Fort Jackson, I had seen mostly blacks and some uneducated whites doing the hard work and the rest of the whites doing easy work. At Fort Sam Houston, I watched as mostly the white boys got assigned to the best military bases, including the Pentagon, while the blacks were sent to tough places like Fort Hood. At Fort Hood, I observed many white boys being reassigned to administrative jobs, while well-educated blacks were assigned to manual-type duties like the motor pool. I said, "No, sir, I have to fight. I hope you will respect me for what I have to do. I hope you will stay out of my way."

Frustrated and apparently disgusted with me, he shook his head and slowly walked back to his area of work. I felt some pity for him but understood his subservient attitude. After all, I knew my parents and my grandfather would probably have given me the same advice. I understood his conditioning because I too had harbored many of these same feelings. I felt fortunate that I had made a transition and was prepared to take a bigger risk. To be honest, I had been a little surprised by my attitude and my willingness to take this major risk. While I would have never admitted it, I was starting to question the wisdom of my action. Yet I felt driven and simply could not accept things as they were without trying to change them.

That night I lay in my bunk pondering what options I could pursue. It then hit me, the words that Mrs. Williams used to repeat to me. "Nathaniel, if you want to work for change, remember that the pen is always mightier than the sword." That's when I decided it was time to use the pen. It had worked for me in college, why not now? The next day, without a word to anyone, I started composing letters to President Dwight Eisenhower; to my U.S. Senator from Georgia, Richard Russell; to my congressman, James C. Davis, who represented my county in 1959. I also wrote to Congressman Carl Vincent, who was a member of the influential military affairs committee, and to the general of the army. In these letters I laid out my case and pointed out how I felt the army was making improper use of my talents. The letter included my name, rank, serial number, and my duty station. I emphasized how I had been misled earlier at Fort Sam Houston by having been promised advanced medic training and how they assigned me to Fort Hood instead. I talked about my background and pointed out that I was offered no hope of any adjustment at my base. I identified the areas where I felt I could function and make a real contribution to the army. I signed and mailed the letters. After all the letters were gone, I mentioned to several soldiers in the barracks what I had done. Some of the younger soldiers thought it was great, but the older ones were not happy. All of them were uneasy enough to say that they didn't want to be too close to me when the "shit hit the fan." I knew I had stepped across the line and that it was possible I would pay a hefty price, but I was convinced I was right, and was prepared to suffer the consequences.

A week went by and I had not received a single reply. Actually, I was so naive that I thought each person would write me individually and either encourage me or intervene on my behalf. It was on a Wednesday of the second week after I had mailed the letters and I was in tank-driving school, when the officer in charge ordered me to report to his office. When I arrived, he appeared quite uneasy and wasted no time telling me I was to return to my barracks, shower, change into my dress uniform, and report to the company headquarters and the captain's office on the double. I followed his orders exactly. I arrived at the company headquarters and was directed by the company clerk to have a seat. When I asked the company clerk what was going on, all he would say was the captain was meeting with his staff on a matter of some urgency. Of course, it didn't occur to me that I was that matter of urgency. After about forty-five minutes, I was ordered into the captain's office. To my surprise, I found the captain and his entire staff, including my first sergeant. I was directed to sit in the one vacant chair in the room. The captain sat behind his desk, and the others flanked him on either side.

Boy, this didn't feel too good. I was starting to wonder if I was about to be subjected to a court martial and if it was procedure to require the wearing of your dress uniform, but I knew that I hadn't done anything bad enough to warrant a court martial panel. Then I spotted a bundle of letters on the captain's desk and recognized one of them as having been written by me—one of those I had sent to the high brass. Now I understood why I hadn't received any replies to my letters. They had all been sent on to the captain. It dawned on me I might be in over my head. I was starting to sweat and realized that what I had been told earlier about the "shit hitting the fan" was already starting to splatter and smell.

The captain began separating the stack of papers on his desk into five separate piles. It was then that I understood the military process. Each person I had written to had passed the letter to the next level to be handled. Every person in the room sat quietly and waited nervously for the captain to let the hammer fall on my head. Frankly, I had concluded that it was not whether the hammer would fall, but when it would fall.

Finally, the captain began, "Private Lee, you have caused quite a stir within this chain of command, stretching from the president's office to my office. On my desk I have all your letters written to the president and all the others, each of which has been sent back down through the chain of command, including the base general, all communicating a basic directive 'to place this soldier' in a position commensurate with his education, training, and skills. This matter needs to be resolved immediately and reported back through the command to the proper authorities. Those are my orders direct from the base commanding officer who wants this matter dealt with immediately."

"Private Lee," he continued. "I am a very unhappy man, and you, soldier, you have put me in a very uncomfortable spot. So what do you have to say for yourself?"

Nervously, I said "Well, sir, I really didn't mean to create problems for you or anyone, but I did request reassignment and you gave me no reason to believe this could or would be worked out at your level. So I used the only weapon I had, so to speak, to try and get some action."

Only the captain talked while the others sat and listened attentively. After a while I was wondering why they were there, but it wasn't long before I understood.

The captain continued, "Private, we have worked out a reassignment for you and these folks are here as my witnesses, just in case you decide to misinterpret what I am about to say. I am directed to reassign you to either the personnel office or the Mental Health Clinic, where you will be placed in the position as a social work technician and will perform the duties and responsibilities required of that position. Private, you will be under intense scrutiny, and if you make just one mistake or create one more problem while assigned to this post, appropriate action will be swift and sure. Is that understood?"

I replied, "Yes, sir."

"Private," the captain said, "You will be relieved of all guard duty and all KP and your hours of work will be from 0800 hours to 1700 hours, Monday through Friday. You will also have all your weekends free and will receive a permanent weekend pass." I couldn't believe what I was hearing. This sounded too good to be true. I tried to brace myself for the downside. I didn't have to wait long before the other shoe dropped. At this point, the captain leaned forward on the desk with a look of sadistic pleasure on his face as he continued, "Private Lee, you will physically remain under my command. You will continue to be assigned to this company while on temporary duty to the mental health group. Therefore, you will remain in the same barracks, you will sleep in your same bunk, and you will face the same men every day. Of course, these men will know that you were the one who felt you were too good to serve with them and get your hands dirty."

At this point I interrupted, "Sir, may I speak?"

"Speak, soldier," the captain said. "Sir," I stated, "I never said I felt I was better than these men, nor have I ever indicated my unwillingness to serve with them. I have always taken the position that I was not being used to my fullest potential."

"I hear you soldier," said the captain, "but it will be hard for these men to watch you lay in bed sleeping while they have to roll out for reveille at 0500, or to know they are pulling guard and KP while you are relieved, or that when they are required to leave the company area and go to the field for maneuvers, you will be basking in the comforts of the base in a warm and cozy office. How do you think they will interpret it when you get up and put on your dress uniform and go to a comfortable office, while they are dressing in their work fatigues headed for a dirty motor pool to sweat in the heat and freeze in the cold? I think they will feel that you are too good to work with them."

The captain was presenting a horrible picture, and I was obviously showing signs of uneasiness. "Private Lee," he said, "I would not want anything to happen to you, so you might want to rethink this assignment before I return this document certifying your placement." He then picked up another document and said, "Now, this document says that you decided to waive your request for reassignment and certifies that you will remain in this company and perform the duties assigned to you. For your safety and future, we, your command team, suggest that you sign this one."

For a second I hesitated, but then said, "Captain, with all due respect to you and the command team, I reject your offer and request that I be reassigned on temporary duty to the Mental Health Clinic."

There was no reaction from the others, but the captain looked around the room in disbelief. Obviously agitated, he turned to me and said, "In that case, you will report to your new duty station at 0800 tomorrow, Wednesday, and check in with the officer on duty. You are dismissed, soldier."

I said, "Yes, sir," and left.

As I walked back to the barracks, I knew I had to do some damage control with the other guys. I went in and found several of my buddies anxiously waiting for me to report. I was a little apprehensive, but I shared what had taken place in the captain's office. I fully expected some negative reaction, but to my surprise all of them gave a jubilant response. Several said, "You took on this man's army and you won. Do you have any idea what that means? It means that you have proved that if you're right and you have the courage to stand up for your convictions, you can get justice in this army." I was very relieved at their overall reaction. I was not rejected by a single member of the barracks. I became somewhat of a folk hero. I had taken on the system and won. After work, we celebrated my victory.

The next morning, I reported to the Mental Health Clinic. During the next few months, I worked hard to master my duties and to gain the confidence of my superiors. I was finally satisfied and felt no further need to challenge my assignment. I was thoroughly enjoying my new job and found the experience challenging and personally rewarding. I was actually enjoying my military experience. However, I was not free of temptation and was soon drawn into another controversy. Once again, I found myself headed down a treacherous path.

9 From Coffee to Korea

One Saturday morning in August 1960, I decided to visit the town of Killeen. Dressed in civilian clothes, I spent most of the morning walking the streets window-shopping. I decided to stop at the local drugstore for a cup of coffee. I didn't anticipate having any problem, but after a while it was obvious that I was being ignored. Then I remembered I had been told that the only thing black soldiers should do in Killeen, Texas, is to catch a cab and leave town.

I eventually realized that I was not going to get served, but I was determined not to let them continue to ignore me. I was also starting to get very angry, but knew I needed to maintain control. After waiting a few more minutes, I got the counter girl's attention, and asked for a cup of coffee, only to be told, "We don't serve your kind in here." I snapped back, "What kind am I?" "You know," she said, "colored." I said, "It's fine for me to give two years of my life serving in the army and that doesn't qualify me for a lousy cup of coffee?" The manager came over and asked if I was a soldier and I replied that I was. His next remark startled me when he said, "We have an understanding with the base that if any of you Negra soldiers give us any trouble, we just call the MPs and they will handle the matter. If you don't leave now, I will call the MPs." I knew he was serious and I was in no position to force the issue. As I got up to leave I said, "Don't fire until you see the whites of my eyes, but take a good look because I will be back." I still don't remember what I meant by that statement, but it sounded good at the time. I left and went directly back to the base.

During the next five days, I spent hours pondering my response to the drugstore incident. I knew that sit-ins had occurred in Greensboro, North Carolina, and other places and that Dr. Martin Luther King had been arrested for various protests in the South. I talked with several of my buddies and persuaded eleven to join with me to launch a protest demonstration. I was careful to select soldiers who held key positions and who were well-mannered college graduates. My idea was to hold a sit-in at that drugstore the following Saturday. I made sure they understood they would be taking a chance and could be punished if things went badly. In spite of that, I was delighted that each one was eager to participate. I was surprised when several of them expressed they had wanted to do something to call attention to the treatment of black soldiers in Killeen. They considered this that opportunity and felt a sit-in could do a lot of good. I felt this was an effort for black soldiers only. I just didn't feel it would be fair to subject white soldiers to such possible consequences.

I contacted several television and radio stations and newspapers. To my surprise, the only reporter who actually showed up was from the *Dallas Morning News*, which was 156 miles away. I was disappointed at the media's lack of interest. The plan was in place to meet at the main gate at 11 o'clock on Saturday morning. Each person had to be "spit and polished" in full military dress uniform. We would walk to the drugstore and quietly take our seats at the counter. The plan was to sit until we were served. I believed that the media could and would expose how black soldiers were being treated while serving their country. It didn't dawn on me that we might actually be arrested.

I had arrived at the post main gate at 10:45 A.M., where a reporter from the *Dallas Morning News* was waiting. He informed me that he had been dispatched to cover the event, but that his editor wanted to talk with me before we proceeded. We walked to a nearby telephone booth. He dialed the number and handed me the telephone. I stepped inside the booth and closed the door, which was instantaneously yanked open. There stood two MPs and a person in civilian clothes. One MP directed me to sit in the back seat of the car. By this time, all of the other guys had arrived and were watching. The person in the civilian suit walked over and asked if everybody was there to participate in the sit-in. I was shocked that they knew all about our plan down to the smallest detail. Everybody answered yes. We were all informed that we were being taken into custody. We were not told anything, but by now I was growing real concerned about where we were being taken. We were taken through the front doors at battalion headquarters and eventually escorted into a large room. One of the MPs said we were there to meet with the commanding general. It was starting to sink in that we had been brought to the woodshed. This time I had struck a real nerve but had no idea until later just how much I had irritated the power structure.

Eventually, the general's aide entered the room and directed that we follow him. We went through several huge doors and entered a massive office.

The walls were oak-paneled, the carpet was so thick it felt like I was walking on air, and the furniture was the most beautiful I had ever seen. There was a gigantic desk and the American flag positioned behind a beautiful, black leather, high-backed chair. I had only seen pictures in magazines that looked like this office.

We were directed to sit in twelve chairs, which had been arranged in front of the desk. I was directed to a special chair, which was right in front of the general's desk. As we sat waiting, I fantasized for a few fleeting seconds about someday working in such an office. I actually believed it might be possible, then suddenly the door opened and we were called to attention. The general went directly to his chair and said, "At ease," indicating we could sit down again.

He was a heavy-set, balding man who wore green fatigues and combat boots. He asked, "Which one of you is Private Lee?" I slowly and hesitantly raised my hand and responded, "I am, sir." "Well, Private Lee," he said, "Tell me what this is all about." I shared the story of my experience at the drugstore counter and how this had provoked me to feel the need take some action to try and fight discrimination.

As I talked, the general listened intently, focusing his eyes squarely on me. When I finished, he asked the others if they wanted to make any comments. Only one person, a lawyer who worked in the adjutant general's office, indicated that while he had not had any such experience, he felt we could not allow such actions to go unchallenged. When he finished, the general turned to me again and asked, "Why do you think you have the right to challenge the practices of this community? After all there is more than enough for you to do on base, and I know there is more than enough coffee to satisfy your needs in the food outlets. Your actions only make things difficult for some of the older soldiers here."

I responded, "Sir, it's not just the coffee. My concerns are based on principle. How can I, a soldier who is willing and ready to die for my country, accept being treated like a second-class citizen and knowingly allow any practice of discrimination to go unchallenged? I'm sorry, sir, but I believe it is my responsibility to fight segregation, prejudice, and discrimination wherever I find it, just as it is my duty to defend this nation against outside attack."

He then turned and scanned the others in the group. I could tell several of them were starting to get nervous. The general spoke again, saying, "Now, I am willing to overlook this stupidity you exhibited today if you assure me you will not engage in or instigate any protest demonstrations now or at any other time as long as you are on this base." He looked at me and asked, "Do I have your word?"

I knew enough about military procedure to understand that the general could confine us to base and place Killeen and the drugstore off limits. I had no idea what the others were thinking. I looked at my friend the lawyer and shook my head to indicate "no" and was relieved when he nodded in agreement. I then turned to the general and said, "Sir, with no disrespect, and I do understand what you have said to us, I cannot give you my word that we will not go to town. The reason, sir, is that we are American citizens, but more importantly, we are American soldiers who are prepared to fight and die for democracy. Sir, we must also be prepared to fight, sacrifice, and die if necessary for access to democracy here at home. I heard what you said about how our actions could make things hard for some of the older soldiers. All I can say sir, is that maybe if those soldiers had taken similar actions earlier, we might not be here in this office today. It is possible, sir, that I would have been served that cup of coffee. Sir, a lot of Negroes have fought and died so we could have the rights and privileges that our democracy is supposed to guarantee every day. So you see, sir, out of respect for those pioneers and so their work will not have been for nothing, we have to go to town this afternoon. We must sit at that counter and we must do whatever it takes to break that barrier and ultimately drink some coffee in that drugstore. Finally, sir, I can't speak for the others, each will have to speak for himself, but as for me I'll go as often as I can as long as I'm here until they serve me at that drugstore counter."

The general was obviously quite upset with me. He then turned to each of the others and asked, "Do you agree, soldier?" I was very proud when each one said, "Yes, sir." With a unanimous response, the general said, "Private Lee, you and all of you are hereby confined to base until further notice. If you try to leave this post and enter the civilian area, which is now off limits, you will be arrested, incarcerated, and subjected to court martial. Do I make myself clear?"

He turned towards me and I responded, "Yes, sir." He continued, informing us that he had placed troops on alert to stop us from leaving the base. He then stood, and we all jumped to attention. He indicated that any further disciplinary action would follow then abruptly left the room. We were all escorted to waiting MP cars and delivered to our respective barracks.

I spent most of the rest of the afternoon lying on my bunk staring at the ceiling and wondering what my fate might be. It was clear I had truly screwed up. It was like I was being driven toward these challenges. It felt as if something inside me just wouldn't let me walk away. I had a comfortable job and really had things going my way, so why did I want to put everything on the line in this place and at this time? I kept telling myself, "You have less than two years left. Do the time, and get the hell out of the army." I did not have any answers, but also I did not have any regrets. Somehow I just felt driven.

It didn't take long for the word to spread throughout the base community about what had happened. Most of my buddies thought I was crazy. At the same time, most expressed their support and thought I was doing the right thing.

Later that afternoon, the older black soldier who had lectured me at the motor pool approached me again and said in disgust, "You gonna ruin things for all of us. You just don't know when to quit." He was very emotional and hostile. I resisted the urge to respond because I knew he was conditioned in a different environment. After a few minutes, he walked to his bunk, sat down, and stared out the window.

I went to the mess hall for an early dinner. When I returned to the barracks, I found the company commander and the first lieutenant waiting near my bunk. The captain said, "Well, soldier, you have really done it this time. I have been ordered to terminate your assignment to the mental health clinic, effective immediately. In addition, I am ordering you to report to my office at 0800 hours Monday. At that time you will receive orders for a new assignment. That's all, soldier." He turned abruptly and walked away. There was no doubt in my mind that this time I was about to feel the full force of the army's wrath. I was very worried, but there was no remorse in my heart.

Some of my buddies speculated about what action would be taken against me on Monday. I thought I could be shipped to another base. There was the slight possibility I could be sent to a foreign post, maybe Korea. I was not too worried about being sent to a foreign post because I had fewer than fourteen months left on my tour of duty. I concluded that, in the worst case, I could be sent back to the motor pool to work on tanks.

On Monday morning I reported as ordered to the captain's office. Waiting for me were the first sergeant, the sergeant major, the first lieutenant, my platoon leader, and the captain. We did not get into the captain's office but rather stood in the company headquarters reception area. The only person to speak was the captain, who indicated he had received a set of orders directing that I was granted ten days' leave, after which I would report to Fort Ord, Oakland, California. There I would be processed and transported to the clearing station located in Seoul, South Korea. I was directed to pack all my belongings and be ready to be shipped out within one hour. I would be transported by military aircraft to Fort Stewart, Georgia, the nearest point to my home. He asked if I had any questions.

Not only did I not have any questions, I did not have any feelings left. I was absolutely stunned. I kept thinking, "This is a bad dream and I will wake up soon." But it was real—the one thing I was sure would never take place was happening to me. They were actually sending me to hell—I was going to Korea.

Once I regained my composure, I asked, "Sir, why Korea?" His response was very curt and icy cold, "Since you think things are so bad here in America, we want you to see how bad things can really get in other places. Also, we know you can't cause but so much trouble in Korea. When you get back to America from Korea, maybe you'll appreciate living in the United States."

I didn't say anything, but I was thinking, "I don't regret anything I've done and, given the same set of circumstances, I'd do it all over again."

I was escorted by a military policeman to the airport for a flight to Atlanta. I was swished away so quickly, I didn't have a chance to bid farewell to my barracks mates or any of my buddies.

I asked the MP taking me to the airport if he knew what had happened to the other eleven soldiers. He indicated we were being shipped to different bases overseas. Most of the others were going to places like Japan, the Philippines, and Germany. He told me, with some glee, that I was the only one being shipped to a "hardship" post. He said, "Boy, I think you are in for one hell of a tough tour of duty over there. I sure wouldn't want to be in your shoes." I felt a tinge of disgust with myself for disrupting what might have been smooth sailing through my tour of duty at Fort Hood. I found it hard to believe that I had been dumb enough to throw away a cushy opportunity. I was starting to question my own sanity.

But then I remembered a comment my grandfather used to make when he had gotten himself into a messy situation. He said, "Son, when you step in a pile of cow manure, no sense in cussing the cow. Just accept the responsibility for not looking where you were walking and then go clean up." I felt my grandfather's presence and felt some relief in remembering his words. The plane took off shortly after I was aboard. As we ascended, I watched Fort Hood gradually disappear from sight and knew that my life would be changed forever. I arrived angry at the army and was now leaving angry at myself. I had no idea what the future held for me and was not sure I would be prepared even if I knew. I felt life had once again handed me a lemon and I needed to try to make lemonade.

10 North to Camp Casey

I spent a week with my family in my hometown of Lithonia. During my leave I had time to reflect on my actions, and I started to have regrets. I promised myself that once in Korea I would conform and accept and follow orders without question. Shortly after arriving at my duty station, that promise was quickly forgotten.

My parents were concerned about my going to Korea and were very unhappy about what I had done to cause this reassignment. My mother expressed hoped I would learn to stop "misbehaving." She could not understand why I was so "hell-bent on stirring up trouble" instead of just doing my job. I tried to explain that I didn't think it was right to be denied access in a free society. I felt I was being sent to Korea for fighting discrimination. I reminded my mother of the time my grandfather had refused to give up his seat on the textile plant bus where he worked because of his pride and the fact that he was sick of being pushed around. I assured my mother that I would never make a special effort to find trouble or create conflict. I did tell her that I would always make noise about discrimination and would always make whatever sacrifice was necessary to fight segregation and oppresion. I told her that my grandfather's action taught me that, whatever the price, you must take a stand. I didn't satisfy my mother, but she said that she understood and would pray that I would "meet with no harm."

The day before I was scheduled to leave, my dad pulled me aside and said, "Son, I never got in the army. I really didn't want to go in the army. Mostly I didn't want to go overseas. Now you're going a long ways from home. Your mother and I won't be nearby, although you don't need us to protect you. You will be on your own." He said that he realized that I had basically been on my own since I left for college, but he felt this was different. If things went wrong in America he could come and help, but if things went wrong in Korea he would not be able to get there. He expressed a sense of pride in my willingness to take a stand and then be willing to accept the consequences of my actions.

My father then reached out and hugged me, which is the first time in my life I can remember being hugged by my dad. There was never any doubt that my father loved me, but men didn't hug—they just did not exhibit emotion. Fathers simply did not express love or any form of softness toward their children. Fathers were supposed to be tough and to set and enforce limits and be great disciplinarians. So it was quite gratifying to feel this emotional connection with my father.

The next day, a Saturday, Dad drove me to the Atlanta Airport to catch a plane for Oakland, California. It was about 4 P.M. when the plane lifted off the ground. As we flew over downtown, I fixed the image in my mind of the Atlanta skyline. Finally, the plane rose above the clouds, and I had no further visual contact with my home.

I spent the night in Oakland and was processed the next day, Sunday. Early Monday morning I boarded a Flying Tiger plane, along with other soldiers and some family members bound for Korea. I had been told that with several stops, the trip would take approximately nineteen hours. It would be the longest time I had ever spent on an airplane, and the longest trip I had ever taken.

I arrived in Seoul and was quickly cleared through customs. Eventually, a colonel came to extend us a welcome to Korea and to explain how valuable our service would be to the international peace-keeping efforts. After about ten minutes, I heard my name called and was directed to take my duffel bag and proceed to a bus bound for Camp Casey at Tongduchon. I asked one of the soldiers standing next to me if he knew the location of Camp Casey. "Yeah," he said, "but you don't want to know. Camp Casey is the boil on the butt of Korea. You will be a few miles from the North Korean border, above the 38th parallel, isolated from any major urban area, surrounded by rice paddies, and freezing your ass off in the winter. Other than that, it's a pretty nice place." He said this was his third tour of duty in Korea and his second time being assigned to Camp Casey, mainly because he kept "pissing the brass off in the States." His description of Camp Casey made my heart sink. He then said, "All I can say is that somebody back in the States really wanted to teach you a lesson."

We climbed on board canvas-covered trucks and spent most of the night, with several rest stops along the way, riding on rough roads north towards my new home.

It was early morning when we arrived at Camp Casey, forty miles north of Seoul and eleven miles south of the DMZ (Demilitarized Zone). I was processed and assigned to Company A, the ambulance company, 1st Bat-

Standing guard on the 38th Parallel near North Korea, 1960.

talion, 7th Infantry Division, a medical battalion. I was assigned as an ambulance driver. Once again I felt I was being relegated to a position below my education. It was August, so the weather was mild, but I was issued clothing and gear for a bitter early winter.

The next day I went to the company commander's office to ask for a reassignment. The company clerk denied my request to speak with the captain. Then my luck changed. As I turned to leave, the captain walked through the front door.

He was a tall man, weighing close to two hundred pounds and appeared to be in good physical condition, and to my surprise he was black. The name on his uniform read Ferguson. As he got near, I snapped to attention and sounded off, "Captain Ferguson, sir. May I have a word with you, sir?" He was obviously caught off guard. However, he remained composed and responded, "Soldier, what's your problem?" I asked if I could speak with him in private. This, too, I learned later, was an unusual request, but amazingly he granted it.

Once in his office I explained that my value to the army would be greatly diminished and my talent wasted if I was forced to drive an ambulance. Sarcastically, he thanked me for making him aware of my importance and value to the army and said that I could be assured that he would keep that in mind. He then turned and walked away as he mumbled the words, "Carry on, soldier." Based on his reaction, I felt my fate had been sealed and that I would probably be driving an ambulance. I wasn't sure what to do next, since I was beginning to feel like a cat that had used all nine lives. I decided that I was beaten and had no choice but to commit myself to learning to drive an ambulance. I spent the next week in ambulance-driving school, hating every minute. In spite of my feelings, I worked hard to learn the skill.

Late that Friday afternoon, as activity was winding down for the weekend, Captain Ferguson approached me and asked if I was adjusting to being an ambulance driver. I replied that I was still unhappy and felt underutilized. His response was that he really hoped I would try to make things work because I was walking on thin ice. He said if I screwed up again, I could end up in the stockade. I asked him if he thought I would be punished if I wrote the president about my situation. He immediately said, "You can write the president or anybody else you can think of, but nothing will change your assignment here." He emphasized that both my record and reputation had preceded me to Korea and that any slight mistake would not be treated lightly. "Hell," he said, "I even knew I was going to get you before you left Texas. You are perceived as a troublemaker, and they wanted to make sure that you went down under the command of a black captain. You've got a star on your ass shining so bright that everybody is taking aim at you."

I said, "Sir, I just can't take this lying down."

"You're right," he said, "but if you don't do it sitting down, your ass is going to be locked up. Carry on, soldier." We saluted and he walked a few feet away, then stopped suddenly, turned, and said, "Private Lee, come to my office at 0900 hours Monday."

I simply said, "Yes, sir." Although I had no idea what he was thinking, I was delighted that he had something in mind.

I was waiting when Captain Ferguson arrived on Monday morning, carrying his patented swagger stick. As he walked by he used his stick to motion me to follow. Once in the office, he directed me to take a seat. Then he proceeded to chastise me for thinking so highly of myself and believing I deserved some special treatment because I had finished college. Then he said with emphasis, "Hell, I finished college." He further suggested that if I kept walking so close to the line I would eventually cross it and find myself in deep trouble. He then said, "There is something about you that is likable. You are one lucky bastard." He explained that soldiers had been sent to the stockade for far less challenging actions than mine.

At the same time, he was quick to point out that he felt he had better rescue me. He said he was convinced that if he didn't do something to help calm me down, I would be in the stockade within six months. He then asked what position I thought would make me feel better utilized. I replied to say some "office work" where I could use my educational skills. He wondered if I could type. I told him that I had taken typing in high school and could type eighty words per minute. He wondered if I knew how to manage a filing system. I responded that I had never done it but was sure I could learn. Would I be willing and satisfied to be company clerk? "Absolutely," I replied with a tinge of joy in my voice.

He then said, "If you can assure me that I won't be embarrassed, I'll request you be reassigned as assistant company clerk and be ready to take over when Specialist Gerald Wicks, my company clerk, rotates back to the States in three weeks."

I was so pleased that I was about to wet my pants, but I didn't want Captain Ferguson to know, so I remained cool. In my most calm voice, I replied, "Sir, I would be honored and pleased to be your company clerk."

With a Korean soldier who was a close friend and buddy, Camp Casey, South Korea.

He said that I should continue in ambulance-driving class until further word and that he would let me know as soon as he could work things out.

To my surprise, when I reported for reveille the next morning, the first sergeant told me to report to the office and begin my duties as assistant company clerk. From that point on, life in Korea was peaches and cream.

When I reported for duty to the Company A headquarters, Mrs. Williams' words rang in my head, "I can't guarantee you will ever get an opportunity, but I can guarantee that if you ever do, you will be ready to seize it." It finally came, I was ready, and I seized it.

Gerald Wicks was a heavy chain smoker and drinker. At day's end he would go straight to the beer garden and drink up to three large pitchers of beer. Most mornings he would report with a hangover, and many times he could barely function. Although he was still physically in Korea, he had mentally checked out. First Sergeant Wilkins was aware of this and began assigning more and more responsibilities to me. There were days when Wicks did not report for duty until mid-morning. By the time he departed, I had long been performing as the full-time company clerk. The day he left, I was formally transferred to the company clerk's desk. I felt vindicated and was determined not to screw up this situation.

I credit Captain Ferguson with having rescued me from a terrible fate in Korea. I have tried to contact him many times over the years, but have never been successful.

The next year in Korea for me was filled with activities and gratifying experiences. I spent time learning the culture and trying to learn to speak the Korean language. I made special efforts to rub shoulders with middle-class Korean families, many of whom welcomed me into their homes.

I expanded my involvement in extracurricular activities on the base. I hung out at the service club many nights and would join others singing while someone played the piano. One of these times, Leonard McCullough was playing the piano and asked me to join his musical group as vocalist. I took the stage name of Baron Lee and performed every weekend with the Len Mack Trio. Leonard played the piano, John Boone the drums, and Reggie West the saxophone.

Someone drifting into the NCO Club on the American military base in Tonduchon on a Saturday night in the fall of 1960 would have seen me step up to the microphone and launch into "A Foggy Day," "Blue Moon," "That Old Black Magic," or any of several other romantic ballads. I was twenty-five years old. People back in Lithonia, Georgia, U.S.A., would have been amazed to hear those suave and sophisticated songs coming from the boy they had come to know as Nat Lee. I had come a long way from singing in church and with family gospel-singing groups and the Bruce Street High School chorus.

Most of the performances of the Len Mack Trio and Baron Lee were at service clubs throughout Korea, and they took place mostly on weekends. We became so popular that Special Services offered to send us on tours to other military bases. Since it would require that I extend my tour of duty, I rejected the offer. The drummer was a professional musician who performed in Las Vegas and was already booked for a year upon his return. He was so impressed with me as a singer that he invited me to join him upon my discharge. I was flattered and excited about this opportunity, but by the time I returned home, I had lost interest and had decided that I did not want to be an entertainer and perform in Las Vegas.

Following one of my performances with the Len Mack Trio I was invited to perform in a play sponsored by the Hourglass Service Club Theatre. I had been a good actor in high school and college, but had not been in a real play since graduating from college. I played a lead character in Thornton Wilder's *The Matchmaker*, which received rave reviews. On opening night General Pachler, Camp Casey's commanding general, attended and joined the cast for a postperformance reception. This was the first time I had been

Teaching typing to soldiers in South Korea.

in the company of a general since leaving Fort Hood. General Pachler was very impressed and complimentary of my acting skills.

I also spent two evenings a week teaching typing to soldiers. The program was offered under the auspices of the University of Maryland. I rotated three classes of twelve men each through the program during my stay in Korea.

I joined the Korean International English Institute and taught English proficiency to Koreans. Through this experience I learned to speak Korean on a limited basis, and my students learned to speak English. Korean was a difficult language to learn, yet this was one of the most rewarding experiences I had during my entire stay in Korea. A high point of my stay in Korea came when I was invited, along with a select group, to visit the presidential palace. I thought how ironic it was that I had never visited Washington D.C., my own national seat of government, the Capitol, or the White House, yet here I was, standing on the grounds of the national seat of power in Korea.

I even completed writing a novel, entitled *Trouble*. Most of the writing was done on weekends and nights while I was on duty. It told the story of

With faculty associates at the International English Institute, South Korea.

a very light-skinned black girl who returned to a southern town and met a dark-skinned lawyer. Most people in town thought she was white and, as a result, while the lawyer was on a date with her, he was arrested and tried for violating the law forbidding interracial dating. The story ended in the courtroom when the sheriff became so angry he fired a shotgun, killing the girl.

My time in Korea ended up being far more enjoyable than I had imagined possible when I first arrived. When I first arrived in Korea, I was told that, when the women start looking good, it meant I had been there too long. That did not work for me because when I arrived in Korea the women already looked good, and when I was ready to leave, the women were still looking just as good. My tour of duty felt much shorter than the actual eleven months I spent there. On July 16, 1961, I boarded a Flying Tiger bound for Oakland, California, where I was honorably discharged on August 19, 1961. I took my first flight on a jet plane from San Francisco to Atlanta.

When I left home I was a very immature young person, but I was coming home a mature man. When I left the South it was segregated and oppressive, and when I came home to the South it was still segregated and oppressive. There was, however, one difference. The civil rights movement was developing and I could feel the restlessness growing among blacks. In spite of these challenges, I was glad to be home. I was glad to be back in America. For the first time I began understanding clearer what Little Brother Cooksey had felt. At the same time, I reasoned that my time in the military was necessary to guarantee my freedom as well as my right to protest bad conditions. More importantly, it was to make things better for future generations and make it possible for my children to enjoy a life full of greater opportunities. I was proud to have served and pleased to have made the sacrifice for my country.

11 From Savannah to North Carolina

Shortly after being discharged from the army and returning to Lithonia, I accepted a job in Savannah, Georgia, as a juvenile probation officer. I was hired at the grand salary of $315 per month, which I later learned was $100 less than the salaries of the white probation officers. In addition, my caseload was more than double because black youth were being incarcerated at an alarming rate, many for very petty acts. While I viewed Savannah and the job as a temporary stop on my professional journey, I dedicated myself to initiating new efforts to saving as many of these juveniles as possible. I worked closely with the public schools, the local boys club, and local community-based groups. Our efforts had some impact, judging from the reduction of incarcerations during my three years in Savannah.

Savannah contributed to stabilizing and anchoring my life. I arrived as a single man and soon became a very popular bachelor. I was not looking for a wife, was seeking no serious relationship, and had absolutely no thoughts about marriage and a family. But like the song says, I fooled around and fell in love. Lillian and I met during one of my visits to an elementary school where she was teaching. I thought she was a very beautiful woman and was immediately attracted to her. On the other hand, she would later confess, she viewed me as a playboy "who thought highly of himself." A few days later, our paths accidentally crossed again, this time at the local bowling alley. We had an opportunity to engage in more extensive social conversation. We had several more accidental meetings at the bowling alley over several weeks. Finally, I felt comfortable enough to ask for a date. Before agreeing, she wanted me to know that she was a divorcee with two small children. Initially, this gave me pause. But since we were only dating casually, I was comfortable. As we spent more time together, we found we enjoyed each other's company—and we shared at least one mutual pastime, bowling.

The more we talked, I found her to be both charming and highly intelligent. I was even more impressed that after her divorce she had returned to school, earned her bachelor's degree, and was pursuing her profession as a public school teacher. I felt this was the kind of woman who would make a good partner. Without a doubt I was not wrong, because we have fit together like a hand in the right-sized glove. At the same time, Angela, Ricky, and I developed a loving and close relationship. While I questioned my own readiness to become a parent, I found many other reasons that this union would benefit all of us.

After dating for slightly over a year, the time seemed right. Lillian and I were married on November 24, 1962. I was twenty-eight, and she was twenty-seven. We bought a small, four-room house for $4,000, with monthly payments of $33.07. We were bringing home a combined total income of $517 a month. We were able to meet our obligations, but had very little disposable income. Therefore, our entertainment consisted of weekly visits to the bowling alley, and occasionally a movie. We were very happy, though far from being satisfied. I had dreams of going to graduate school to earn a master's degree in social work, but we were uncertain how we could finance it.

Fortunately, I had befriended a wealthy white woman, Mrs. Lillian Spencer, who was a benefactor for a children's home known as Greenbrier. She was also the wife of one of the wealthiest and most powerful men in Savannah, Captain Frank Spencer, a shipping magnate who was a noted early civil rights advocate. Captain Spencer had been one of the organizers and an early member of the Savannah Chatham County Council on Human Relations. He frequently corresponded with Dr. Martin Luther King Jr. and other civil rights leaders. Mrs. Spencer was a social worker who constantly prodded me to pursue a graduate degree in social work. She often introduced me to prominent out-of-town professional friends who would visit on occasion.

In early 1963 she invited Lillian and me to attend a talk by Dr. Frank Porter Graham, whom she called "Dr. Frank." I had never heard of him and had no idea who he was, but I felt that Lillian and I had better attend, if for no other reason than to humor Mrs. Spencer. I found out later that she thought Dr. Graham might be persuaded to help me get enrolled at the University of North Carolina.

Lillian and I were the only two blacks in attendance at an event that was held at the Savannah Public Library. As we shared this experience with friends later, we often said, "We felt like two flies in buttermilk." It was certainly not an everyday occurrence that a black couple would be in the room with whites in 1963 in Savannah, Georgia. But there we were, sitting in the front row as nervous as two cats on a hot tin roof. The quiet in the room was suddenly broken by loud yelling from an older white woman who had just arrived. She immediately began protesting our presence, pounding her cane on the floor and saying loudly, "What these niggers doing here? I will not sit in the same room with any niggers. Get them out of here!"

Captain Spencer went to the lady and said in a very audible voice, "You either shut up and sit down or get out." We were later told that this lady was an acquaintance of Mr. and Mrs. Spencer and was a known racist. Most of the others in the room were embarrassed and made special efforts to apologize for the woman's behavior. It was ironic, because Dr. Graham's speech focused on the struggle for human rights in the world. At the time, he was a United Nations mediator for the United States and had served as president of the University of North Carolina before he was appointed to the United States Senate to fulfill an unexpired term due to the death of Senator J. Melvin Broughton. He ran for election in 1950, but was defeated in a vicious campaign filled with racial overtones. In 1963, Graham was going around the nation giving his talk "The United Nations in Perspective and Hope."

After he talked that night, Lillian and I were introduced to Dr. Graham, who was a gracious and pleasant man. Though he was small in stature, his presence dominated the room. We engaged in a short pleasant conversation. His graciousness and insightfulness made quite an impression on both of us. We wanted to know more about him and his life's work. But he was more interested in us. He was especially interested in my future plans. He had been told about my desire to attend a graduate school of social work and understood I was thinking about applying to the University of Georgia. He wondered if I had considered the University of North Carolina. My response was that I had not. He then quipped that I should at least apply to "a real great university." I learned later that this was an inside joke, since there was a long dispute as to which university was the oldest established state university.

As we ended the conversation, I told Dr. Graham that the chance of my attending any graduate school was more of a dream than a plan, since Lillian and I had two children and no money. He encouraged me not to let money be a deterrent to advancing my education. Then he said, "If you decide to apply and if you can get accepted at UNC, I will commit to helping you find the money to pay the tuition." Not only was I shocked, but for the first time I saw a glimmer of hope that this could be my golden op-

portunity. In spite of my optimism, I still held on to a tinge of doubt. I just didn't believe this would actually come true. In addition, I anticipated that Dr. Graham would return to North Carolina and I would become a distant memory.

The next day, I mentioned this conversation to my boss, James Niedermayer, the director of the juvenile court, and to my surprise learned that he was a graduate of the UNC School of Social Work. He was excited that I had met the great Frank Porter Graham and urged me to apply. When I shared the substance of Dr. Graham's promise, he told me that he was still a powerful influence at UNC and that he could deliver on any promise he made. He emphasized that Dr. Graham was one of the most honorable men in North Carolina and among the most respected. He assured me that if Dr. Graham promised to help, I could be confident he would keep his word.

After that conversation, I went to the library and spent many hours researching the UNC School of Social Work and Dr. Frank Porter Graham. I was impressed to learn how he had built the North Carolina University system into one of the most respected institutions of higher learning and that he himself had been a victim of racism when he lost his senate election bid in 1950. The more I learned, the more I realized I had been in the presence of a great man.

I knew there wasn't enough time to get admitted to UNC in September 1963, so I started planning for 1964. Following Dr. Graham's advice, I submitted my application to the School of Social Work at UNC in February of 1964. In addition, I submitted applications to the all-black Atlanta University and to the University of Georgia, my original choice. The University of North Carolina was the first to respond. I was directed to take the Graduate Record Examination and complete the Miller Analogies Test. I had never heard of either and therefore had to scurry to both understand the tests and find out where to take them. By mid-April 1964, all my documentation was submitted.

On May 5, I received a letter from Mrs. Barbara Cleveland inviting me for an admissions interview in mid-May. We did not have enough money for me to spend a night in a hotel, so I left Savannah by bus at 11 P.M. on Thursday, traveled all night, and arrived in Chapel Hill early on Friday morning. I used the bus station restroom to change clothes and then set out to explore Chapel Hill and the campus.

This was my first time in Chapel Hill and the first time I had visited a major university campus. I asked a policeman for directions to Alumni

Hall, where I was to meet Dr. Arthur Fink, dean of the school, and Mrs. Cleveland, the admissions director.

I left the interview feeling pessimistic about my chances of being admitted, concerned that I hadn't made a good impression. Several weeks passed with no word. Meanwhile, a white colleague at the juvenile court, James Shimkus, who had applied after I did, had already received his letter of acceptance. Once that happened, I was sure I had not been accepted. So while I was waiting for my rejection letter, I decided to apply for a position with the U.S. Job Corps.

I called Captain Spencer to tell him I was doubtful of my acceptance. He said he had talked with Dr. Graham, who advised that I should be patient because "these decisions take time." In the meantime, I had decided to write Dean Fink, requesting financial aid, "if I were accepted for admission." Finally, on May 30, I received a letter of acceptance. That night we celebrated.

I contacted Captain and Mrs. Spencer, shared the good news, and asked if they would let "Dr. Frank" know. Captain Spencer's reply was, "Don't fret, he already knows." Since we had no indication that I would be approved for financial aid, Lillian and I had borrowed two thousand dollars from the Household Finance Company, enough to consolidate our debts so we could live on Lillian's income alone.

In early June, I received a letter from the dean informing me that I had been awarded a two-thousand-dollars-a-year fellowship. This was followed by a letter from the housing department assigning me to room 405, Connor Dormitory. I was ecstatic.

However, my excitement was short lived. A letter dated June 18, 1964, arrived from Dr. Earle Wallace, associate dean of the Graduate School, informing me that my scores on the Graduate Record Examination were unsatisfactory. My heart sank for a few seconds. The next line brought major relief as it read, "The provisional nature of your admission to the Graduate School has been continued. You will not be asked to retake the examination; satisfactory achievement in courses taken in one or more semesters at the University will remove this condition." This felt like history about to repeat itself, since I was admitted to Fort Valley State College under similar conditions. On the other hand I had survived Fort Valley and was confident I would survive in the School of Social Work. No matter. I was prepared to take my chances and felt confident I could meet the requirement. I never could confirm it, but I always felt that Dr. Frank probably helped in securing this arrangement.

As I rejoiced over my new beginning, I couldn't help but feel that my destiny was being fulfilled. I could not know then what a destiny it would be.

On September 15, I left my wife and children in Savannah to begin classes on September 16. I was apprehensive because this would be my first real experience in an integrated environment other than the controlled environment of the military. I was both anxious and excited about my new challenge in life, but ready to meet it head on.

My adjustment to the rigorous schedule of the School of Social Work was relatively easy. I was one of only two black students among a class of forty, including my former colleague in Savannah, Jim Shimkus. Jim and I had worked in the same office area at the Juvenile Court for three years, but we had not been friends. We had always been courteous to each other, but had seldom spoken, and never socialized. However, once on campus at UNC, Jim and I became good friends. When it was time to elect officers for the Student Social Work Association, Jim encouraged me to run for vice-president and offered to manage my campaign. I was hesitant at first, but then decided I had nothing to lose. There was no opposition candidate, so I won by acclamation. The following year I was elected president.

I did not anticipate staying in Chapel Hill after graduate school, but I was interested in becoming acquainted with the community. Each Sunday I visited a different black church but had not determined if I would join any one church. I was intrigued when Ralph Cauthen, a classmate, invited me to visit his church, Binkley Memorial Baptist Church. I had never set foot inside a white church for a formal service. But when I went with Ralph, I was highly impressed with the Reverend Robert Seymour, the senior pastor. I thought his sermon was very thought provoking. But what impressed me most was the length of the service, one hour, as opposed to close to two hours at most black churches.

However, I did not go back to Binkley until I brought my family to Chapel Hill in 1965. Lillian had no interest in joining a predominantly white church, so she resisted making a visit. Finally, she agreed to attend one service and was instantly impressed by Dr. Seymour. She was touched by the warm, welcoming atmosphere. Our visits to Binkley became more frequent, but we did not decide to join until I had accepted a position offered to me by Duke University. By then, we had bought a house on the east side of town, near Binkley. Once these decisions were made, Lillian and I decided joining Binkley was the right choice for us. We had become very comfortable worshiping in a white congregation and were impressed that Binkley had been organized as the first Baptist church in the area to welcome blacks as members. Before us, there had been only one black couple, B. T. (Thal) Elliott, a medical school student, and his wife, Edith, a social worker affiliated with the church. However, by the time we decided to join in 1965, we were the only black family in the church. Later I would become Binkley's first black deacon.

We also felt that joining Binkley would give our children an opportunity to interact with children of different cultural and ethnic backgrounds, which we hoped would better prepare them to function in the broader society. They wouldn't have to endure the stress of making the transition as we had done. Attending Binkley and living in student housing was Lillian's first experience in a desegregated environment.

It was at Binkley that I met Dean Smith for the first time. He was on the rise but had not yet become a famous coach. I recall when he was first introduced to me as Dean Smith. I thought "Dean" was his position title at the university. So I naively asked, "Dean, now tell me what department do you head up?" He just smiled, and before he could respond, someone else said, "He heads up a department called basketball." I was embarrassed and apologized. In spite of that awkward start, we developed a strong friendship, and as time went on Lillian and I both developed a close relationship with the basketball program.

Our initial involvement was to help Dean Smith recruit UNC's first black basketball player, Charlie Scott, in 1968. From the late sixties until Dean's retirement in the nineties, Lillian and I participated in recruiting many of the basketball team's players. Our oldest daughter, Angela, became one of Dean's key assistants and worked with the players' families.

In her role as surrogate mother, Lillian also became a link with the parents. At the end of each basketball season, she would prepare a huge southern-style dinner for the players, which she called a soul food feast. Even after graduating and having gone on to play professionally, many players, upon returning to Chapel Hill, would ask her to make them a carrot cake.

Lillian and I invested countless hours in volunteer service in our new community, Chapel Hill. I personally began a program called Saturday Academy to provide tutoring to struggling black students at Chapel Hill High School. The academy met for five hours every Saturday at the First Baptist Church for two years. When the program ended, all the students had graduated from high school and enrolled in college. I continued to be active in many different ways in the community.

12　The Oath of Office

In the five years following my arrival in Chapel Hill as a student, much happened. I completed my master's in social work at UNC. Lillian and the children moved from Georgia to join me in Chapel Hill. In 1966 I accepted a job at Duke University and moved the family into a house in Colony Woods. I had made history by being the first black elected as mayor in a predominantly white, southern town. I was truly living a dream which Dr. King espoused.

At 7:30 P.M. on May 12, 1969, I was sworn in as mayor of Chapel Hill, receiving the gavel from the outgoing mayor, Sandy McClamroch. The Town Hall chamber was packed with media and spectators. My mother and father were not able to attend, but my sister and several brothers did make the trip from Georgia. After the oath was administered, I took my seat to deliver my official inaugural speech. I had crafted the speech to try to set an upbeat and positive tone for my administration and to reemphasize the commitments I made during the campaign.

I wanted to highlight my commitment to unify all parts of Chapel Hill: the comfortable and mostly white segment, the poor and mostly black segment, and the university. I said that as mayor I would never respond to issues based on race but prioritized on need. Many of the problems in the black community had been ignored for too long. I pointed out how this neglect had resulted in unpaved streets in that part of town, poor sanitary service, little or no access to sewage lines, and a lack of recreation facilities. As an example, I cited the Mitchell Lane embarrassment in the black section, where a big ditch had been used for years to dump garbage such as old tires and used oil. Black leaders had repeatedly pleaded with the town to fix the problem. I proposed to place this item on the agenda at the next board of aldermen meeting, where I was given full support by a majority of the members.

The second point I emphasized in my speech was that, within one month, there would be an office for the mayor set up in the Town Hall and that it would be staffed. I wanted to send a message that things would be different and that I intended to be an activist and productive mayor.

The next day I met with the town manager, Robert Peck, to work out details for setting up the office. We did not get off to a good start, which indicated that I could not expect much cooperation from him. The manager informed me there was no room in Town Hall and that the best he could offer was an office for the mayor in a downtown office building. I said that would not be acceptable because the public expected to visit the mayor at Town Hall, not some external office building. His response was to remind me that he took directions from the board of aldermen, not the mayor. At that time, the board met every two weeks, which meant it would be two weeks before this matter could be resolved. During the interim, I spoke with board members, who at the next meeting unanimously directed the manager to find space to set up an office for the mayor in Town Hall and to do so immediately. Within a few weeks, I opened and occupied the first official mayor's office in the history of Chapel Hill.

Being aware that the board would be required to adopt a town budget

Taking the oath of office for mayor, May 12, 1969; administered by the town clerk, David Roberts. Photograph courtesy of Billy E. Barnes, Chapel Hill.

before June 30, 1969, I wanted to know what was being proposed. At this first meeting with the manager, I got another surprise. I was told that the town could not adopt a budget until the university had an opportunity to review what was proposed. As directed by the North Carolina State Legislature, the university historically made a contribution to the town in exchange for certain municipal services. It turned out that the mayor and manager customarily went to discuss the proposed budget with the university's vice chancellor for budget and finance. I had no choice but to accept this custom and attend the meeting. The experience was demeaning to me as mayor, and I viewed it as disrespectful to the town. I could not accept that a legitimate municipality had to discuss its budget with a university before it was discussed with the elected official town board. I managed my feelings at the meeting, but as we returned to Town Hall, I told the manager that as long as I held the office of mayor this custom would not be honored again. I did propose a compromise: we would allow the university to discuss our budget, but the meeting would take place at Town Hall and not on the campus. The board unanimously adopted this change.

The budget was adopted on time, including a thirty-thousand-dollar

Surveying depressed areas of Chapel Hill as mayor.

allocation to the mayor's office. My request for a salaried position for a mayor's assistant, however, was not approved. Instead, the town manager was directed to provide support through existing staff to the mayor's office. That arrangement was not working because I was at my Duke office all day, thus leaving the office uncovered. Complaints began to mount. Fortunately, I was asked whether I would accept a UNC Divinity School student by the name of Andy Little as an intern. I was delighted because he did not require a salary and would commit to a one-year placement. Andy came on board in the first week of August 1969. In 1970 a position of assistant to the mayor became salaried and adopted as an official part of the budget for the first time in town history. Andy stayed on until 1972.

During the first four months after taking the oath of office I focused on organizing a commission to develop plans to bring public transit to Chapel Hill. There was a lot of public interest and support and everything progressed extremely well. I had the full cooperation of the Board of Aldermen. My popularity was growing each day. I was getting great press and I was in high demand for appearances around the state and the nation. Then the unthinkable happened. I made my first major political mistake, which plunged me into despair.

On September 12, 1969, I was speaking to black elected officials at a Washington conference on how to tap federal funds to support community-based programs. During the question-and-answer period, I was asked whether in North Carolina the attitude toward accepting money from the federal government was different from most other southern states. I said, "We are not much different. You can't expect a southern state like North Carolina, which has a southern-Democratic, bigoted governor who refuses to appoint one black person to a major commission, to aggressively pursue federal funds to help towns such as Chapel Hill." The instant I finished my response, I felt a sinking feeling in my gut. However, I hoped maybe the national press would not highlight the statement. Unfortunately, a reporter from the Charlotte, North Carolina, newspaper was in the audience. He approached me later and inquired as to whether I meant to accuse Governor Scott of being a bigot. Instead of backing up, I indicated that was exactly what I meant. The next morning the headlines in the Charlotte newspaper read "Black Mayor Calls Governor Bigot."

Early the next morning, the first telephone call I received was from my wife at 6 A.M. She asked, "What the hell did you say about Governor Scott?" I explained what had happened. She was not amused and told me in forceful terms, "You have screwed up and need to get your behind home immediately." The next call I got was from Billy Barnes, who continued to advise me, as a friend. Billy was quite shaken and reinforced Lillian's directive that I should get home immediately. As I talked to each one of them, I admitted I had screwed up. I realized I probably had ruined myself and embarrassed my friends. I screwed up by making that kind of open statement and being that forcefully critical of a governor without understanding the implications. I realized I should have kept my mouth shut because there was nothing to be gained other than notoriety from making that kind of accusation against a sitting governor. But being a good friend, Billy indicated that I had big problems in Chapel Hill and in the state. He was not gentle saying that the fallout was hitting the state like a firestorm. Within a few seconds, it seems, I had done more to divide the state than most people could have done in years. As a result I had also played into the hands and the minds of the black power activists, who were just jumping for joy. On the other hand, the more responsible blacks, like John Wheeler, president of the Mechanics and Farmers Bank of Durham, were embarrassed. These were my supporters in Chapel Hill, who were angry that I would go out and do something so stupid as to pick a fight with the governor. The governor, like many throughout North Carolina, did not hold Chapel Hill in high regard because of its "liberal" reputation, and my comment didn't help. It also didn't help that Governor Scott had attended Duke and NC State as an undergraduate, and not UNC.

The flight between Raleigh-Durham and Washington, D.C., was only fifty minutes, but on this day it seemed more like five hours. I had a lot of time to ponder what my fate might be in the end. I realized that my political future was hanging in the balance and my position at Duke University might also be in jeopardy. On the ride home, I kept playing my comment over and over in my mind, trying to determine how I could have been so reckless and irresponsible. There were two events that I think subconsciously influenced my action.

The first occurred in July 1969. I had been invited to New York to be a judge in the first Miss Black America contest, held at Madison Square Garden. I met Floyd McKissick, at the time national director of the Congress of Racial Equality, who was also a member of the panel of judges. Floyd invited Lillian and me to join him and his wife the next morning for breakfast at his home. I didn't know Floyd personally, but was familiar with his historical achievements in North Carolina as the first black person to receive a law degree from UNC–Chapel Hill, as a civil rights lawyer, and as a civil rights leader. We were honored to have been invited and were delighted to accept his invitation.

During that breakfast he said he was curious about my experience as mayor in North Carolina and whether I was optimistic that I could survive. I expressed strong optimism about my future. But then Floyd emphasized that I shouldn't be too naive. He wanted me to realize that my appointment as a faculty member in the School of Social Work at UNC was being "derailed" by people in high, powerful positions. He went on to point out, "You are a threat and therefore any tactic that can be used to keep you down and discredit you will be used. You've got to find a way to kick some ass. The best thing you can do is to get in a fight with the governor and put him in an embarrassing and defensive position. You got to let the people know that he's a bigot and that the university is discriminating against you because you got elected. They wouldn't do this to a white guy. You have to keep white folks on the defensive."

I was most uncomfortable with Floyd's tone and his advice. Consciously, I rejected that tactic, because I felt it would work for a civil rights leader but not for an elected head of a municipality. I knew my behavior had to be different and my responses had to be controlled and reasoned. Yet when I reflect on that conversation, I am convinced my conversation with Floyd was resting in my subconscious and may have triggered my outburst during my speech at the conference.

Second, I was influenced by my perception that Governor Scott had played a major role in blocking my appointment at the School of Social Work. I had been interviewed for the job before I was elected mayor. I had been confident of being approved and had served notice to Duke University that I would be leaving. But the day before I was to speak at that conference in Washington, I received a call informing me that my appointment had been withdrawn. No reason was given. This meant I might be without a job, which made me very angry. Incredibly, at the precise time I was giving my speech in Washington, the governor had agreed, and my appointment at UNC was being approved by the full Board of Trustees.

When I got off the plane at Raleigh-Durham, I fully expected a throng of press to be waiting at the gate and was quite relieved when there was none. I quickly made my way through the terminal, retrieved my car from the parking lot, and drove to Chapel Hill. I met Billy Barnes at the Glen Lennox shopping center, located on the south side of town. I parked, immediately jumped in Billy's car, and was promptly whisked away. Billy had already written a draft apology, which I read and approved. I thought it set the right tone. Instead of holding a press conference, I sent the apology to Governor Scott via telegram and released copies to the press.

The next day the media, especially the *Charlotte Observer*, carried a story headlined, "Mayor Lee Apologizes for Calling Scott Bigot." I was further quoted as saying "I am sorry for having referred to Governor Scott in a manner which, in retrospect, I now consider unwarranted and ill-considered."

The Chapel Hill newspaper ran a cartoon depicting me in an airplane seat with my foot stuck in my mouth and an attendant standing nearby asking, "Did you have a nice trip to Washington, Mayor Lee?" At the next meeting I apologized to the Board of Aldermen, and a few weeks later the furor had died down and I was able to get on with trying to be an effective mayor.

I requested an audience with the governor, feeling I should apologize in person. I was never turned down, but was told that with his tight schedule it would be difficult to arrange. I believed this was a polite way of rejecting my request.

A few days later, state senator Ralph Scott came to Chapel Hill to give a speech at the university. At his request, we met on campus and I got my first lesson in Politics 101. Senator Scott, the governor's paternal uncle, was one of the most powerful legislators in the state. I had not met him and actually knew very little about him as a person or as a legislator. I didn't know what to expect from him and was most relieved when he told me he felt I could have a bright future in politics. He further indicated that this experience might ultimately be viewed as more positive than negative. "You probably don't realize it," he said, "but going public and apologizing shows more strength than weakness." I confided that I wanted to apologize to the governor in person, but was unable to get an appointment. He agreed to make arrangements for me to meet with him because he felt if I got to know the governor I would understand he was not a bigot. Two weeks later, I met the governor in his office for my allotted fifteen-minute appointment. He accepted my apology and indicated the remark was not that insulting, saying, "I've been called worse things."

Governor Scott reminded me that we first met in 1968, when I was one of three speakers at the state Democratic Party convention. He was lieutenant governor and a candidate for governor. He remembered that at the end of my speech, I had appealed for unity among Democrats and challenged the convention to "add black power to white power, divide by green power, and multiply by political power, which would equal people power." He admitted he was so struck by that line, he occasionally used it in speeches during his campaign. Governor Scott was very gracious and most courteous during our visit. I left this meeting with feelings of relief and optimism. He even suggested that we move beyond this mistake and work together to make things better for all North Carolinians.

I had managed to overcome my problems with the governor, I had been reassured by Duke I still had a job, the town governing board had accepted my apology and given me a public vote of confidence, and most of my friends and supporters were cautiously standing with me. But my problems with the black activists were just beginning. While most black leaders felt I had acted responsibly, the militants and activists, along with some white liberals, took to me to task. I was accused of caving in and behaving more like an Uncle Tom than a proud black man. One of the black newspapers called me a "sell-out" and referred to me as an "Oreo" (that is, black on the outside but white on the inside). I even felt the wrath of many of the black students on the campuses of UNC, North Carolina Central, and Duke. This anger was stirred by the Black Panther group, which was being organized at these institutions. Stokely Carmichael, a national black militant, had been invited and paid to speak at Duke University. He decided also to visit the campus of North Carolina Central University, where many of the UNC students attended his talk. His fiery speeches simply fueled the actions of students at all three universities. One direct outgrowth of this speech gave rise to an organization at UNC called the Black Student Movement. There were many demonstrations on campus and marches from the university to and through the black section of Chapel Hill. I was the target of many of their speeches, often referred to as the "Uncle Tom mayor" or the "Oreo mayor." The police were always on edge and often wanted to break up demonstrations. I was determined that as long as demonstrations were peaceful, we should allow them to take place without police interference. Some on the police force felt it sent a wrong message to play a passive role. But the chief of police, Bill Blake, supported this position and stood his ground.

Just when I thought I was free to start implementing my campaign promises, I was sidetracked once again by another unexpected challenge. Never in its two-hundred-year history had the University of North Carolina experienced a worker strike of any kind. But that would change in November 1969, when the Lenoir Dining Hall food service workers went

Early meeting with Governor Robert Scott, 1969.

on strike demanding higher wages and improved working conditions. A national union joined forces with black militants to encourage the workers to set up a picket line. Black militants and black power advocates flocked to Chapel Hill to participate in the protest. The Chapel Hill police force was dispatched to maintain peace, but with strict instructions not to break the picket line. University President Bill Friday and I agreed to work closely together in order to maintain control of the situation. We were concerned that if Governor Scott sent in the highway patrol or National Guard, it would fuel a reaction that could become violent. We discussed our strategy with UNC Chancellor Carlyle Sitterson, who signed off on the plan and asked that President Friday and I take the lead and keep him informed. President Friday talked with the governor, who reluctantly agreed to go along with our plan, although he was very uncomfortable. He reminded us that North Carolina, being a "right-to-work" state, did not have to honor picket lines, and warned that if things went badly he would not hesitate to flood the campus with state troopers or the National Guard.

There was extreme tension on the picket line and on campus, and we knew any little spark could create an explosive situation. Many of the students decided to participate by walking the picket line, which added to our concerns about maintaining control. President Friday and I worked hard to keep channels of communication open between all parties, the workers, the university, the governor's office, and the police department. In addition to the chancellor, we recruited the faculty chairman Dr. Fred Cleveland, Dr. Paul Guthrie from the School of Business, Alderman Joseph Nassif, and Police Chief Bill Blake to meet with us each morning for daily briefings. Our strategy was to have the Chapel Hill police present at the strike scene, but not to interfere with the picketers as long as they were peaceful. Many people were involved trying to bring the strike to a speedy and peaceful end. For more than thirty days, Bill Friday and I were up from 4 A.M. until late evening. Many people were trying to negotiate, trying to persuade the food service contractor to make an offer of settlement. We worked hard to keep sides from becoming polarized. The workers themselves were ready to settle and would have accepted almost any gesture of goodwill from the contractor, but neither Saga Food Service nor the union would budge.

One big sticking point was a demand by the union that several workers fired during the strike be rehired. The company said no. The university offered to underwrite the cost of reinstating the workers, but the company still said no.

President Friday and I became concerned when we learned that an attempt was being made to organize three thousand black students from across the state to come to Chapel Hill on December 9, 1969, for a rally labeled "Black Monday." I was worried about the increased clashes between the picketers, including several black UNC students, and the police. One incident earlier had already resulted in sixteen black UNC students being arrested and at least six slightly injured. The police were growing tired and on edge, and I was not happy that the union leaders were becoming more aggressive. But I was even more upset that the company was making little effort to compromise. The governor's office, having gotten the same information about the student protest, called to ask if we wanted the State Patrol and National Guard mobilized. President Friday and I agreed that would be a bad idea. The governor accepted our decision to stay the course and use only the local police to maintain order, but again warned us that we were accountable if things went wrong. Meanwhile, I began to realize that frustration was growing and the police were becoming the target. Some of the black militants were trying to provoke the police.

A mediation panel, which had been appointed by Chancellor Sitterson and chaired by Dr. Paul Guthrie finally negotiated an agreement on all issues except the rehiring of between fifty and sixty workers who had been discharged at the beginning of the strike. This was one of the major demands of the union, but the company dug in its heels and refused to discuss the matter. President Friday, the chancellor, and I appealed to the company to relent and agree to the rehiring, but the company refused, citing insubordination as the reason for the firings.

I started to believe that as long as we kept the police patrolling the campus the company would feel no pressure to settle, because nonstriking workers were still reporting to work. I suggested that maybe if we pulled the police off the campus, that might leave the company feeling unprotected and force a settlement. At first, this was not accepted as a good suggestion, but after considerable discussion the idea was accepted. It was clear this was a high-risk response and if things did not go well, I could be badly hurt politically. Alderman Joe Nassif and I explained the plan and rationale to Police Chief Bill Blake, who also thought it was not a good idea. However, he did call a meeting with Major Coy Durham, his second in command, and laid out the strategy. There were expressions of strong disagreement by the officers, who felt this would be a recipe for disaster. I was accused of betraying the police department and told that I would regret taking this action. I finally made it clear that I was not there to ask permission, but rather to inform them of my decision. I then gave the directive to pull the police off the picket line.

President Friday was to make sure that Governor Scott knew the plan. Needless to say, he was not happy. I learned later that he was so sure this would not work, he moved several hundred highway patrol officers to a secret staging area near campus. That night Chief Blake called and appealed to me to back down. Nevertheless, as planned, at the end of the shift the police were pulled off the campus.

When picketers arrived the next morning, there were no police in sight. They were confused, union leaders were surprised, and the company officials were in shock. When the company inquired about police protection, the chief told them of my decision. Later that morning, I was asked to meet with a company representative, who urged me to reverse my decision. I informed him that with the company showing no real commitment to expedite a settlement of the strike, our police could not spend endless days protecting their stubbornness.

Later in the afternoon, the company requested a meeting with Dr. Paul Guthrie, chairman of mediation panel, and agreed to all terms, including rehiring the workers, increasing the workers' hourly wages, and improving other working conditions. On Tuesday, December 9, 1969, at 3:30 A.M., a contract was signed between the union and the company. After one month, the strike was over, and all the employees reported back to work.

As it turned out, students did come to Chapel Hill for the planned rally, but only about four hundred showed up. Instead of a protest, the rally in front of the UNC student union building became a celebration. President Bill Friday and I had rolled the dice and, fortunately this time, won.

The *Chapel Hill Weekly* had initially criticized me and accused me of going beyond my role as mayor by interfering with the police department and injecting myself in university affairs. In a newspaper article, the company referred to me as a black power advocate. But on December 10, 1969, I was flattered by an editorial that appeared in the *Chapel Hill Weekly* praising me, President Friday, and others for our success in settling the strike peacefully. Following is an excerpt from that editorial:

> The person to whom we would like to pay special tribute is Chapel Hill Mayor Howard Lee. Probably more than any other individual, he was responsible for keeping violence to a minimum.
>
> For almost a month, daybreak found him where the action was in the area of the picket lines. In the small hours of virtually every night he would be in the midst of one conference or another, seeking some solution and trying to keep the lid on.
>
> Mayor Lee literally drove himself to the brink of physical and emotional exhaustion, at incalculable cost to himself personally and professionally and to his family.
>
> He showed great courage and as it turned out, a rare understanding of the situation in deciding to withdraw Chapel Hill police from the strike scene. As much as anything else, this drew the teeth from the strike and paved the way to final settlement. If violence had broken out on the picket line, he would have been hard put to defend his decision.
>
> As a sustained effort in the public interest by a public official in Chapel Hill, Mayor Lee's performance is unmatched.
>
> Without the dedicated service of both Dr. Paul Guthrie and Mayor Howard Lee, God know what might have happened.

Bill Friday and I always had high regard and a deep respect for each other. But after spending this month together, our relationship evolved into a very special friendship, which continues today.

I have on occasion thought that Dr. Frank Porter Graham, who contributed so much to the development of the university and was such an icon in Chapel Hill, would have been pleased with how President Friday and I handled the strike. I have often wondered if his hand was somewhere in this outcome. Because he is responsible for my being in Chapel Hill and because he was Bill Friday's mentor, it seems right to give him credit for positioning both of us to make the kind of difference he would have made in the lives of these workers and this university.

I was hoping this would be the most difficult crisis I would face as mayor. But that was not to be. One night, someone set fire to the Chapel Hill School System central administration building. At first I was sure that members of the Black Panther group were the perpetrators. But when the evidence was assembled and the investigation was finished, it was shocking to learn that the act had been committed by five black Chapel Hill High School students.

This was major news in North Carolina and especially in Chapel Hill. The community atmosphere was very volatile and fragile. I was under intense pressure to make an example of these five students, both from inside and outside the black community. Many people concluded that I would find a way to give the students a slap on the wrist and not push for heavy punishment. Even many blacks called to urge me not to be too hard on "the kids." Most thought that if anyone would understand why they would commit such an act it would be me. I even heard some say that if these kids were white and the mayor was white, they would get off lightly. I listened to all the various expressions. I then held a news conference and stated, "As long as I am mayor of Chapel Hill, no one, regardless of skin color, age, or gender, will be excused for committing any destructive act. Therefore, as mayor, I intend to push for these youth to be punished to the full extent of the law." I wanted to send a strong message to the community that anyone who engaged in such destructive acts in Chapel Hill would feel the full wrath of the mayor. During my three terms, we did not experience any more vandalism.

In spite of the many distractions during my early days in office, I had great success following through on most of my campaign promises. One of the first concerned municipal buildings. Chapel Hill voters had approved a bond referendum to construct a new municipal building and council chamber. But no action had been taken to solicit bids for the construction. In September 1969, the town manager was directed to move this project forward immediately and make sure there would be an office for the mayor.

The second campaign promise was to improve the town's recreational programs. Chapel Hill had only a part-time recreation department, a part-time director, and only one recreation facility, which had been built by the federal Work Projects Administration program in the thirties. The town had made no effort to improve the facility because the whites who were not permitted to use university facilities had access to a private swimming pool and the country club facilities. My pledge was to expand recreation facilities and decrease dependency on the university.

Anne Barnes and I had discussed developing a comprehensive recreation plan that would include open space, parks, tennis courts, ball fields, and a central recreation facility. We knew it would take time and money to accomplish all this, but I was determined to make a start toward fulfilling this campaign promise. At my request, the board agreed to give greater authority to the recreation commission, to authorize the hiring of a full-time executive director, and to confirm Anne Barnes as the commission chair. Within two months, the late Henry "Hank" Anderson was hired as director and became the first black administrator in the history of Chapel Hill.

The board also agreed to an increased budget for the Recreation Department, and I committed to aggressively apply for federal funds to help underwrite the expansion. Under Anne's leadership a proposal was submitted to the U.S. Department of Housing and Urban Development, which awarded a sixty-seven-thousand-dollar federal "Legacy of Parks" grant. This was the town's first-ever grant from the Department of Housing and Urban Development. The grant permitted the acquisition of land to be preserved as open space, walking trails, and parks. We were soundly criticized for purchasing one parcel, located in a sparsely developed area on the north side of Chapel Hill on Weaver Dairy Road. Today, Cedar Falls Park is often referred to as a "mini" Central Park; it is completely developed, with ball fields and tennis courts, and is one of the most used facilities in the county. As fate would have it, the first grant I approved when I became secretary of the North Carolina Department of Natural Resources was to Chapel Hill for the development of Cedar Falls Park. By the time I left the office as mayor, a comprehensive recreation development plan had been adopted.

In spite of the obvious need, Chapel Hill had not sought to expand public housing for many years. There were only sixty units of public housing, and a waiting list of more than two hundred families. There was a five-member housing authority, chaired by Edwin Caldwell Sr., a well-respected and longtime black leader. There was, however, truly a negative

Meeting with young people at a neighborhood center. Most were members of the Mayor's Youth Council.

attitude towards providing housing for low-income residents. In order to begin to meet this need, a group of churches had pooled resources and requested a permit to build a sixty-unit housing project known as Inchuco, from the first letters of the name Inter-Church Council. Most of the occupants would be black. The Board of Aldermen had not granted a building permit because the project would be located near an upscale, all-white, middle-class neighborhood. Even with strong community support, each time the request was presented to the board there would be a tie vote and Mayor McClamroch would vote no. I had promised that if I were elected mayor, the project would be approved and that I would work hard to expand affordable housing. In July 1970 the request was again brought before the Board of Aldermen. As before, there was a tie vote. As mayor, I cast the deciding vote, approving the building permit. The housing units were constructed and occupied within one year.

I held meetings with several developers who were encouraged to work with the housing authority to develop affordable housing proposals. By the end of my first term, public housing units had been expanded to more than one hundred. When I took office as mayor, the housing authority director was part-time. The board approved my request to expand the position to full-time. The late Mrs. Gloria Williams, who had been the part-time director, was hired and became the second black public administrator in the town of Chapel Hill.

In June 1970, the *Chapel Hill Weekly* newspaper published a very positive article, complimenting me for a successful first year in office. But one major initiative was still incomplete. During most of my first term as mayor, I was determined to fulfill my most ambitious promise: to establish a public transit system. This was one promise I was determined to keep, and it was the one promise that became the most difficult to fulfill. There were many who thought my time could have been better spent working on less controversial problems. But I believed that a long-term investment in a transit system would yield great dividends.

By 1970 I had convinced the Board of Aldermen to establish a thirteen-person Transit Planning Commission. George T. Lathrop, a faculty member of the UNC Planning Department, was appointed chairman. George had a strong background in urban transit planning and had played a key role helping me develop my transit platform. The commission consisted of members from the business community, the university, and the neighboring town of Carrboro.

At my insistence, the commission rushed to develop a plan before May

Evaluating the need for improvements in neglected areas of Chapel Hill.

6, 1971, the date of the next local election, in which I would be running for reelection. Because I was proposing to partially fund the system from property tax, a referendum had to be submitted for a public vote. The remainder of the financing was to be generated from the university and the federal government. Some members of the commission, and many of my politically wise friends, thought this was dumb idea. As one of my friends put it, "No right-thinking candidate runs on the same ballot with a tax increase or big tax-spending projects." But I felt I wanted to rise or fall on bringing public transit service to Chapel Hill. I insisted we proceed.

To enhance the possibility of the referendum passing, I wanted to demonstrate the value of a transit system. I persuaded the Board of Aldermen to appropriate fourteen thousand dollars to buy five used buses from Atlanta and arrange with the private management company that had been operating the university buses to also operate the town buses. In March 1971, two months before the municipal election, amid great fanfare—and heavy criticism from the business community—the first buses rolled out.

The effort turned into a disaster. People were not flocking onto the buses, so the system was losing approximately two thousand dollars a week. To make matters worse, the buses were in such poor mechanical shape that they constantly broke down. After seven weeks, the fourteen-thousand-dollar budget was depleted and the system had to be shut down. This occurred just one week before the referendum vote. On Election Day, even though I was reelected with 64 percent of the vote, the bus referendum went down to defeat in both Carrboro and Chapel Hill. In Carrboro, the vote was 65 percent against, but in Chapel Hill, the referendum lost by only one vote.

I was surprised and disappointed, but also encouraged. Losing by only one vote in Chapel Hill energized me to try again. I asked the commission to go back to the drawing board and develop plans to put the question before the people in the 1972 elections. The vast majority of the commission members vehemently disagreed, as did my supporters on the Board of Aldermen, who suggested that more time was needed if the plan was to be successful. I was persuaded to allow more time and seek broader community input. I was convinced the voters in Chapel Hill wanted a public bus system, but had my doubts about the support in Carrboro. Therefore, I urged that we eliminate service to Carrboro and develop a system to serve only Chapel Hill and the university. The commission worked and prepared a referendum, which was voted on in the fall 1973. This time it was approved by 65 percent of voters.

Finally it happened. In August 1974, UNC Chancellor Ferebee Taylor and I cut a ribbon and launched the first official Chapel Hill Transit System. Within a few months, the Chapel Hill system ridership was second only to Charlotte. This was the crowning achievement of my administration. The Chapel Hill Transit System today is one of the more successful systems operating in any town in North Carolina. Hundreds of people flock to the buses because they realize it is more economical to "ride the bus and leave the driving to others." Each time I see a transit bus rolling down the streets of Chapel Hill, I feel a sense of pride and am honored to have had a hand in making it happen.

Because I had won my 1971 reelection by an impressive margin, many black leaders were encouraging me to think about running for a higher office. I really wanted to test my political wings outside of the comfort zone of liberal Chapel Hill, but I was not sure I could be successful. Eventually, I decided to test the water.

I considered running for the newly created full-time office of lieutenant governor. But once I learned that Jim Hunt from Wilson, North Carolina, would be one of the several candidates running for this office, I realized the two of us would be competing for the same vote. Jim and I had become allies during his days as president of North Carolina's Young Democrats Club

Launching the first Chapel Hill bus service, 1971.

and I didn't want to get into a primary with an ally of mine. Before making the final decision about running, I went to see Terry Sanford, my friend and mentor, who took time from his own campaign for president to consult with me. Terry confirmed that Jim was the candidate of choice for many of the power brokers who might otherwise be sympathetic to my campaign for lieutenant governor. Besides, he said he didn't think I would have a prayer of winning. He did think I could win a statewide office, such as commissioner of labor. But he also said he felt that if I were on the ticket, Democratic candidates would benefit from an increased black voter turnout.

He encouraged me to visit one of his strongest financial backers, Bert L. Bennett Jr., a wealthy businessman and a strong statewide leader who lived in Winston-Salem. When I left Bert's office, I was sure of only one thing, which was that I would not be running for lieutenant governor in 1972. It was clear that James Baxter Hunt would be the candidate of choice. Bert suggested I think about running for commissioner of labor. I wasn't sure that was the right position for me, but because both Terry and Bert had suggested it I felt obligated to at least give it serious consideration.

Strategy meeting with Senator Edmund Muskie to discuss Muskie's campaign for president in North Carolina.

13 A Run for Congress

Once it was clear that running for lieutenant governor was not possible, I decided to gauge public reaction and possible support for a run for the office of commissioner of labor. I began dropping comments to the press. On September 1, 1971, the *Chapel Hill Weekly* printed a headline, "Howard Lee on the Brink; State Commissioner of Labor . . . or What?" The reporter, Mary Burch, tried to make me commit to definitely running, but I was still not sure this was the right fit. Instead, I indicated I would make a decision by the fall of 1971.

Then another door opened, when the incumbent congressman of North Carolina's fourth congressional district, Nick Galifianakis of Durham, announced he would not seek reelection. This to me seemed a more attractive opportunity than running for lieutenant governor, or commissioner of labor. I immediately began testing the water to determine my level of support.

Speculation about me being a likely candidate for U.S. Congress to represent the most progressive and liberal-leaning congressional district in the state grew louder. At the time, many people thought this was the only district in North Carolina where a black candidate could be elected. It was also believed that I would be the best person to run. However, a legislative move threw these plans into disarray. In the spring of 1971, the North Carolina General Assembly, in the process of redrawing district lines, decided to move Orange County (including Chapel Hill) from the fourth congressional district and place it in the mostly rural second district. I was surprised by this move and felt it was done to block my opportunity. A decision to run for Congress would pit me against a well-established incumbent congressman, L. H. Fountain of Tarboro. The move dampened my hope for a congressional campaign for 1972. While many believe the lines were redrawn to shut out any chance a black candidate might have of winning, this was vehemently denied by the legislative leadership.

It was rumored that legislative leaders wanted to create a safe district for one of its members, Senator Ike Andrews, from Asheboro. This of course was vehemently denied by legislative leaders. Others contend the district was changed in order to conform to the Supreme Court one-person, one-vote directive. This was how Chatham County, a small rural area south of Chapel Hill, and the home of Representative Andrews, displaced Orange County in the fourth district. (Andrews, in fact, did go on to be reelected to Congress.)

Suddenly my optimistic feelings of higher political office were deflated. On the surface, it appeared that winning in the redefined second district would be impossible. I would not only be running against one of the longest serving congressmen in the state, L. H. Fountain of Tarboro, I would also be running in the most conservative rural district in the state. While I was considered a bright, young, aggressive person with a respectable political background, I didn't believe it would be enough to unseat Congressman Fountain. On the other hand, there were those who believed the congressman was vulnerable and could be defeated. I was not convinced, but did not rule out the possibility of running.

During the newspaper interview with Mary Burch, I spent more time talking about a run for Congress than for the Labor Commission. The issues that excited me most were public school busing, the Vietnam War, poverty in our state and the nation, the need for strong support for educational access and opportunities, and strong Washington representation from North Carolina.

I started believing that having Orange County moved into the second congressional district could be a blessing in disguise. There were several reasons that campaigning in the counties of this district could generate positive fallout. The second district had a larger potential black voting population than even the Research Triangle district. If I were able to persuade black and progressive individuals to run for local offices and if there were an increase in the black vote, then local politics could also be impacted. I began to reflect on my initial decision to run for mayor. It was not just to win but to force the other candidate to focus on and discuss the important issues. Congressman Fountain had not had a serious challenge since being elected in 1952, and for that reason had not been forced to campaign. After serving in the state senate for five years, Fountain had defeated Representative John H. Kerr, who himself had been in Congress for twenty-nine years. Fountain emphasized during that first campaign that this was too long for any man to serve in Congress. In 1972 L. H. Fountain was fifty-eight years old and had served in Congress for twenty years. I felt

I could hammer away on the same theme: "That's too long for any man to serve in Congress." I believed I could force him to come home and campaign, which could be a secondary victory.

I studied the 1968 campaign by Eva Clayton, a popular black woman from Warren County who had challenged Representative Fountain in 1968 and lost by 29,000 votes out of 75,000 cast. She had increased black registration within the district from 11 percent to 26 percent of all voters, and I believed if I could register 10,000 to 12,000 new black voters, I could be victorious. Eva was one of the people urging me to take on the challenge and run. She believed that as a legitimate office holder, I could raise enough money, organize the student population at the university and other smaller colleges within the district, and attract enough active support among many progressive whites throughout the district to win. Eva and several other people thought the stars were aligned by the legislative action that had landed me in the second district. It was believed I could motivate blacks to go vote in larger numbers than they ordinarily would. These were the major factors contributing to my decision to challenge Congressman Fountain.

I was also influenced by the history of the district. This was the congressional district represented by George White, the last black person from the South to serve in the U.S. Congress. White, however, fell victim to the tide of segregation and racial disenfranchisement, masterminded by Democrats, that swept the South at the turn of the century. He was voted out of Congress by the voters of his district in the 1900 election and left office at the end of his term in 1901. I felt I could use that reference to build a strong coalition and motivate voters throughout the district, although I understood the differences between White and me. While some circumstances were so similar, one difference was glaring: George White was a Republican and I was a Democrat, affiliated with the political party that had orchestrated his defeat. As a black modern-day Democrat, I understood the basic problems of prejudice and discrimination George White encountered in 1900. I fully expected that many of those same prejudices would be directed towards me, because racial attitudes in the redrawn second district had not been altered during the preceding three quarters of a century. In 1896 the district ran along the Virginia border into eastern North Carolina farm country and was only 50 percent white, but thousands of black voters were unregistered and too intimidated to vote. In 1972, the district ran along the Virginia border into eastern North Carolina farm country. The district's population was 40 percent black, which was the largest black population percentage of any congressional district in the state. Several rural counties with greater black populations had been dropped in order to add Orange County and Chapel Hill, home of the University of North Carolina. The reconstructed district had a registered voting population of 179,000. The black voting population was now only 26 percent, or 47,000. Nevertheless, as I reviewed the voting population statistics, I was encouraged that I could generate enough excitement to get a big black vote to the polls and make up the difference by running strong in my home county of Orange County.

After considering all the factors, I assembled a small group, drawing on my mayoral campaign committee, which included Billy and Anne Barnes. This ultimately became the core of my congressional campaign committee. At our first meeting, I was given strong encouragement to explore the district and gauge possible support. Once again I felt fate had turned me in a direction I would not have voluntarily chosen, but one I needed to follow. I had to run in this district because it was possible I might make the greatest contribution and give greater hope to more people. I decided this was my calling and I should answer the call. We all agreed it would be an interesting campaign.

In late September 1971, I decided it was time to "fish or cut bait." I set up a series of small group meetings across the district. These original meetings outside of Chapel Hill were attended mostly by blacks, but occasionally a few whites would attend.

Lillian was not overjoyed by the thought I would once again risk my position at Duke campaigning for political office. We both understood I could lose both the election and possibly my job. There was a lot at stake. Our two older children, Angela and Ricky, were in high school and were expected to attend college. Because Duke offered special support to help faculty and staff with college tuition at other institutions, I risked losing this benefit. Our one-year-old daughter, Karin, had been born in September 1970. We had decided Lillian would take leave from teaching for the first two years to spend time with the baby. Consequently, our only income was from my position at Duke. While it didn't seem rational to take this plunge, I was driven and decided the effort was worth the risk.

In October 1971, I held a press briefing in Chapel Hill, where I announced my plans to travel around the second district. I indicated I would make a final decision by December 1971.

I eventually made stops in all eleven counties outside of Orange and met with a mixed response. Many encouraged me to run, while some were doubtful that I would have a prayer of winning. One of my early stops was in Wilson, where I met with a group of ministers and community leaders. Among them was Milton Fitch Sr., who was not convinced I should run and was sure I could not win. He contended there was too much white opposition and too much intimidation of blacks, and that Congressman Fountain was too entrenched. I respected Milton's thoughts; he was affectionately called "Big Milt" because he had traveled the district as a civil rights worker with Southern Christian Leadership Conference (SCLC) and had been actively involved in Eva Clayton's campaign. He wanted me to wait for a better opportunity. He was concerned this would be a setback for blacks, and he did not want them to be disappointed once again.

I was taken aback by Big Milt's advice. No other member of the group challenged him or offered a different view. I simply asked them to hear why I wanted to run and if they disagreed with my rationale I would reconsider. I talked about my preliminary platform, which would emphasize reordering national priorities with increased aid to rural areas, better funding for rural health programs, aid for rural development (especially for farmers), and programs to keep young people at home and stop the exodus of this talent. By the end of the meeting most had started to warm to the idea. Big Milt still expressed doubt about the probability of success, but he assured me that if I decided to run he would do all he could to help me win. Once I decided to run, Big Milt was one of the hardest workers in the campaign and traveled the district many times over helping generate support within the black community. His son, Milton Fitch Jr., took a semester out of school from January through the primary and served as my chief campaign aide and driver. In the other ten counties, I met with strong encouragement and excitement about my being a candidate.

After canvassing the district, it was determined that 56,000 blacks over twenty-one were not registered to vote, despite the fact that in 1968 Eva Clayton had registered over 100,000. I calculated that if I could increase registration and get 60 percent of the black vote to the polls and could draw 16 percent of the whites, I could win.

In late November 1971, I made the decision to run and set news conferences for January 10, 1972, in Rocky Mount and in Chapel Hill. As word spread that I would become a candidate, many around the state were surprised, especially some legislators. Democratic politicians chuckled, thinking it was comical that I would even think I had a chance against L. H. Fountain.

The one person who did not chuckle was Congressman Fountain. Or-

The Lee children, Angela, Ricky, and Karin Lee, 1972.

dinarily, he might have been smug about my candidacy, but with Orange County added to the district, he realized this had all the makings of a tough campaign. For a while rumors circulated that he might retire, but that proved untrue.

As I launched my campaign, I realized I would be carrying a heavy burden, along with the renewed hopes and dreams of thousands of blacks in the district who had felt unrepresented in Congress. Beyond that, even I felt the pressure to conduct my campaign above race and to keep a focus on the issues. After all, I knew I would be watched and evaluated both throughout the state and nationally. Being the first black man to seek a congressional seat since George White in the same district increased everyone's interest. In addition, I was challenging not just any member of Congress; I was challenging the dean of the North Carolina congressional delegation.

During the early days of the campaign, Billy and Anne agreed to work as volunteers, and I hired Dwayne Walls to be my campaign manager. Dwayne was a noted journalist who had authored a book entitled *The Chicken Bone*

Special, which studied the migration of young blacks from the South to northern ghettos. Dwayne did not have very much political experience, but was well respected among journalists and publishers throughout the state. I felt this could help me develop my communications with the media.

By the end of February 1972, the campaign was fully staffed, the fundraising was going well, and I was full-time on the campaign trail. There were campaign headquarters in all twelve counties, and I had appointed two campaign managers, one black and one white. I spent the bulk of my time making campaign appearances in retirement homes, black churches, and college and university campuses and appearing in front of civic clubs. I walked the streets of most towns in the district and made frequent appearances at plant gates. At every stop I hammered on such issues as the infant mortality rate in the second district, which was worse than in Greece and Poland; the per capita income, which was among the lowest in the country; and the fact that that too many young people were leaving the district because there were no decent jobs, and that, in the end, both black and white people were suffering and struggling just to make ends meet. I asked, "When was the last time you saw or talked to your congressman?" Most answered never or a long time ago. I attempted to soften the black power rhetoric by offering unity: "Add black power to white power, divide by green power, and multiply by political power equals people power."

In spite of carrying the burden of being from Chapel Hill, which was considered a liberal haven in most parts of the district, my reception among many whites was cordial, and in a few cases I received praise for making "L.H. get out and meet the people for a change." I challenged Congressman Fountain to a debate, which he promptly turned down. I also launched an aggressive media campaign using radio and newspaper advertisements. I decided to use an aggressive billboard campaign, which caused some problems and created a Catch-22. We plastered my picture on billboards all across the district in an effort to try to motivate black voters. My picture, however, probably only served to remind whites that I was black, and in the long run may not have done much to energize blacks. There were many whites who wanted to vote against L.H., but were not necessarily ready to vote for a black candidate.

I knew I had his attention when he started calling in outside help such as Representative Wilbur D. Mills of Arkansas, chairman of the powerful House Ways and Means Committee, to campaign on his behalf. Fountain had the full backing of the "courthouse crowd," which used to guarantee

News conference with his wife, Lillian, announcing his candidacy for U.S. Congress, 1972. Photograph courtesy of Billy E. Barnes, Chapel Hill.

elections in most largely rural areas and especially in this district. I knew I had no prayer of gaining that crowd, so I had to develop an alternative but potent strategy to counter that influence.

I focused on energizing and motivating preachers as well as high school and college students to be actively involved in voter registration and door-to-door canvassing. I knew if I decided to run, my biggest challenge could be generating support from 15 to 20 percent of the white vote.

I did not run an attack campaign, but did not hesitate to reveal facts. I emphasized that I felt it unacceptable that a congressman who represented a district with a 40 percent black population did not have one black person on his staff.

When the voter registration books closed, more than fifteen thousand new people had been registered. I felt highly optimistic about my chances to win, but one week from voting day I was rudely reminded that my real opposition in the campaign was "black sellouts."

I had realized early that, as I moved into political circles outside of Chapel Hill, instead of being a big fish in a little pond, I was now becoming a little fish in big pond, swimming with many predatory fish, especially political sharks who were eager to feed on little fish like me. According

1970 family portrait.

to some of our surveys, we could win if at least 60 percent of black voters
went to the polls. Obviously, if we knew that, so did Fountain's campaign.
Their strategy was to initiate a vote-buying campaign and start passing
money among black leaders. That is what happened in several counties.
The most blatant case was in the small town of Weldon in Halifax County.
A community organizer named Coley Ashe had attached himself to my
campaign. He was supposedly traveling throughout Halifax, Warren, and
Northampton, counties with a high concentration of black voters, organiz-
ing to get the vote to the polls. He was to arrange for drivers to take voters
to polls and provide them with sample premarked ballots for Howard Lee.
As we discovered on Election Day, he did his job well—for Congressman
Fountain's campaign. Coley had organized and paid off a fleet of drivers

who were instructed to provide rides and hand out sample premarked ballots for Congressman Fountain. We were able to reduce the impact. However, by the time we realized what was happening, many had already taken the money and voted.

On May 7, 1972, primary election day, there were many volunteers and fleets of cars in every county outside of Orange taking voters to polling places. I cast my vote early and then drove thirty miles to Oxford to escort ninety-seven-year-old Hugh "Sandy" Boyd to vote. Mr. Boyd had cast his first ballot in 1896 for George White and was determined, as he put it, "to revisit and correct an historic error."

The night of May 7, I gathered with supporters from throughout the district at the Holiday Inn in Chapel Hill. Cautious but optimistic, I expected to celebrate a victory, but when the final votes were reported I lost the election, with 48 to Fountain's 52 percent of the vote. I was disappointed, but satisfied I had done my best and in the process had left a mark on the district.

The next day, I went to my deserted headquarters and sat quietly reflecting on what I might have done better. There were several small victories. The major victory occurred in Orange County. For several elections, liberals and progressives had been unable to elect a black or woman to the Board of County Commissioners. In 1972 my congressional campaign generated enough votes to elect a black, Richard Whitted, and a woman, Flo Garrett. In several other counties across the district, several blacks, women, and progressives were elected to various offices for the first time. Many who worked in my 1972 campaign for Congress have risen to be successfully elected to various political offices. George K. Butterfield, a campaign field organizer, later became a state supreme court associate justice and finally was elected to the U.S. Congress from the first congressional district. Milton "Toby" Fitch Jr., who was my driver, became a powerful N.C. legislator and later a superior court judge.

When I think of such long- and short-term outcomes, I feel a sense of pride and realize that the investment of time and energy was not lost and is still paying dividends. Through the years I have become more convinced that fate did turn me in a direction I would not have chosen to take, but that's where I was needed and that's where I did the greatest good. Above all it was a personal victory for me that a twelve-year-old black boy could grow up "not just seeing things as they are and asking why, but dreaming of things that had never been and asking, why not?"

I sat alone and kept playing over in my head a line from one of my speeches: "Black and white people should realize that the issues that unite us are more important than the prejudices that divide us." However, I understood that was also true in George White's day. I concluded we have yet to reach this desirable goal of motivating people to unite across racial lines. In spite of losing the election, I was encouraged we were making progress. Since 1972 three blacks have represented the second district in Congress. I am satisfied my campaign was one more small step that pushed us closer to that goal. I had learned from this experience that we must keep learning from history, but never be enslaved by it.

My second-district campaign attracted a lot of national attention, which generated commentaries and articles from such national journalists as Tom Wicker and Bill Anderson. As a result of these articles, I received many speaking invitations, though I accepted very few, because of my job obligations at Duke.

I was delighted to accept an invitation to address the Chicago Chamber of Commerce. I was told that the attendance at the luncheon meeting was the largest crowd in years. The president thought the title of my speech may have generated curiosity. He noted that when a black politician from the South whose name is Lee comes to Chicago and chooses to give a speech called "The South Rising Again," people would be curious and it would attract a lot of interest. The speech was well received.

While in Chicago, I was invited to appear on the Irv Kupcinic talk show broadcast on television station WMAQ. This was the highlight of my trip because I appeared on the show with the actor Scoey Mitchell and Maya Angelou, who was then still a struggling writer.

I spent May and June campaigning for Terry Sanford, who was running hard for the Democratic nomination for president. Terry's campaign was not moving forward because he had lost the North Carolina primary to George Wallace of Alabama and had not gotten a majority of votes in any state. Some of my friends and supporters thought I was wasting time supporting Terry. In spite of these misgivings, I traveled to several states on his behalf. One of the most miserable and unforgettable experiences of that time was flying back to North Carolina from South Carolina on a private twin-engine plane caught in a thunderstorm. The plane was tossed through the air like a toy, and for the first time I questioned the sanity of the commitment I had made. However, I stuck with Terry all the way to the Democratic convention in July in Miami Beach, Florida. I worked the convention hard for Terry, but George McGovern had most of the delegates committed, including the majority of North Carolina's delegates. Terry asked if I would second his nomination, which I agreed to do. The best that accrued to me from this was that I appeared on national television for the first time and spoke at my first national political convention.

When I returned from the convention, I fully intended to return to my position at Duke University and to settle into the mayor's role. But my life was not destined to be that simple. In mid-August 1972, Hargrove "Skipper" Bowles called, asking if I would join his campaign for governor. He wanted me to coordinate his get-out-the-vote campaign, especially among blacks. Skipper also told me that if I played a major role in his election campaign, I would also play a major role in his administration, possibly as a cabinet member. I accepted this challenge and once again I was back on the campaign trail. Most of my emphasis was on organizing a campaign to get out the black vote. Because there was no black on the ticket for a major office, the motivation to vote had waned significantly. For the first time, Republicans were trying to capitalize on black dissatisfaction with the Democratic Party and were making serious and concerted efforts to woo black leaders. Of course, the Republican momentum was being helped along by the popularity of Richard Nixon and the U.S. Senate campaign of Jesse Helms, who was running against Nick Galifianakis. It required a lot of attention to keep the black vote in the Democratic column because Republicans were spending a lot of money in the black community to get out the vote. I worked hard to keep the ranks closed and keep the black vote with the Democrats. Because Skipper Bowles was quite popular in the black community, the defection to the Republican column was quite low. In spite of all my efforts, however, and the hard work of many blacks to deliver the vote to Skipper, it was not enough.

When the polls closed on Election Day in November 1972, Skipper had lost the election. The Democratic candidates for governor and the U.S. Senate had lost. James Holshouser had become the first Republican to be elected governor in seventy-two years, and Jesse Helms had been elected to the U.S. Senate. I was with Pat Spangler, Skipper's campaign manager, when we went into his room to break the news. Skipper and all of us were in absolute shock. I was so close to being in a governor's administration, only to watch it slip through my fingers. The one silver lining in the 1972 election was that Democrat Jim Hunt was elected lieutenant governor. I went back to my job at Duke University and began making plans for my 1973 reelection campaign for mayor.

14 Last Term as Mayor

In 1973 when I announced my candidacy for a third term as mayor, I indicated it would be my last run. I was already quietly exploring a possible run for lieutenant governor. After I won with 89 percent of the vote, I still had many goals I wanted to complete as mayor, and I wanted this to be my most memorable term, without having to manage crisis or controversy. But that was not to be. I and the board of aldermen had grown weary of town manager Bob Peck's failure to move expeditiously to carry out directives. Finally there was no choice but to urge him to resign. I requested his resignation on behalf of the board. He refused to resign and instead insisted the board hold a meeting and publicly fire him. In January 1973, I called a special meeting of the board of aldermen. Five of the six members voted to fire Robert Peck as Chapel Hill town manager. While I would rather not have had this happened during my administration it was something that had to be done.

This action was not universally popular. Several town employees quit in protest, many citizens voiced their opposition, and I was accused of abusing the powers of the mayor's office and attempting to grab power and take over the day-to-day operations of the town government.

Early in my administration, I had promised to appoint a commission to review the Chapel Hill Charter and the manager form of government. In the fall of 1973, when I announced the establishment of the Charter Review Commission and was appointing its members, I was accused of finally setting the stage to replace the manager, with the mayor as administrative head. Initially, I did indicate I would work to create a mayor council form of government, but I quickly determined that was a bad idea. In spite of my disclaimer, many were surprised when the commission's recommendations did not include changing the manager form of government. The commission did recommend that three of my other priorities be implemented. They were to expand the board of aldermen from six to eight members; allow the mayor to vote on all agenda items, not just when there was a tie vote; and have the board of aldermen adopt a committee system. All the recommendations were adopted and implemented.

During my time as mayor, it seemed as if I could not avoid having to manage constant controversial events and one crisis after another. A major crisis erupted within the black community when a historic event was revisited. In 1966 the all-black Lincoln High School was merged with the all-white Chapel Hill High School. Through this process, the Lincoln alumni resented the loss of school tradition, school symbols, and the demotion of leaders as well as concerns about the quality of education for black students. Most accepted Lincoln's lack of comparable facilities; they were more concerned with the loss of passionate teachers, strong discipline, and an unrivaled and award-winning band and strong sports teams.

The Lincoln Alumni Association petitioned the Chapel Hill–Carrboro School Board to correct their error by adopting some of the Lincoln tradition, especially sports symbols. There were threats of protest. As mayor, I was asked to find a way to broker a compromise. I met with school leaders, county commissioners, local ministers, and alumni association leaders. Fortunately, this matter was quietly settled when the school board agreed to work out a plan to integrate traditional symbols.

I had barely breathed a sigh of relief when I was faced with my most difficult task: of having to participate in the destruction of a very important Chapel Hill symbol—removing the "flower ladies" from Franklin Street. A group of six to eight black ladies had set up shop and sold cut flowers on Franklin Street for many years. They were a part of the Chapel Hill image. Students who had bought flowers from these ladies were now grown, and as parents and grandparents of current students would come to town expecting to buy flowers on Franklin Street. The flower ladies were the only group allowed to engage in street vending anywhere in Chapel Hill. Then one day this iconic institution was threatened. A young white woman decided to set up on Franklin Street near the flower ladies and sell handmade leather goods. This created a strong protest from the Franklin Street merchants, who felt that once the sidewalk was open to all types of street vending they would be at a disadvantage by having to compete with these transitional merchants. I understood the concerns but wanted to find a way to keep the flower ladies while restricting others.

The merchants registered such a strong complaint that the board of aldermen decided to enact an ordinance forbidding all street vending, except the flower ladies. I asked the town attorney to draft a tight ordinance to protect against accusations of discrimination. The proposed ordinance, which was adopted by the board, would have banned the display or sale of any goods on the sidewalks with the exception of natural, homegrown, or handmade flowers.

The ordinance was challenged in superior court, and Judge Thomas Cooper ruled against the ordinance. He directed that the exception clause be stricken and that any items similar in size to flowers must be permitted.

After a long and contentious public hearing, we could not find a way to allow the flower ladies to sell without opening the sidewalks to other vendors. Therefore, we decided to forbid all vending on the public sidewalks in Chapel Hill.

This action resulted in a barrage of negative letters sent to me by current students, many townspeople, and a great number of alumni from all over the country. Some letters accused me of being a "Judas mayor" and asked how a black mayor could allow this action to be taken against the flower ladies. In spite of my personal feelings of wanting to protect the symbol, I accepted the criticism and supported the board's decision. This was the most conflicting challenge I faced during my entire time as mayor. In my heart, I resented others trying to infringe on the territory established by these ladies. I felt these ladies deserved to be protected. They had survived a time when opportunities for them were limited. They had used their ingenuity to produce a product and then went out and created a market. Now some "privileged" kids were destroying what these ladies had worked so hard to build up. There were those in the black community who thought it would be shameful if the flower ladies were "kicked off the street" by a black mayor. While I shared many of the feelings expressed, I had an obligation to uphold the law and therefore had to enforce the board's policy of no vending on Franklin Street. The flower ladies were removed.

In the end, all was not lost for the flower ladies. North Carolina National Bank had just built a new building with an open foyer. The bank allowed them to occupy that space at no cost, which kept them on Franklin Street. This was not the perfect or most desirable arrangement, but it did keep the flower ladies on Franklin Street and off the sidewalk.

Serving as mayor of Chapel Hill allowed me to live what had been merely a dream when I was growing up in repressive, segregated Georgia. There were no experiences in my growing up that could have prepared me for being successful in a desegregated political arena. Chapel Hill was the first desegregated environment, other than the military, in which I had lived. I had begun with no political campaign experience, no public office experience, and limited understanding of how government worked or how to manage it. I truly had to learn on the job. Reflecting on my history, I am convinced that I entered the military as a boy and emerged as a man. I entered the office of mayor of Chapel Hill as a man and emerged as an experienced leader.

On May 12, 1975, I held a news conference to make my departure from the mayor's office official. The statement I delivered was designed to capture the spirit and essence of my three terms in office.

My friends, thank you for coming this morning. I have asked you here so that I might announce my decision regarding another term as mayor.

I picked this date, May 12, 1975, not only because it is high time I announced my intentions, but also because tonight it will be exactly six years since I was first sworn in as mayor.

That was an exciting time. But today is far more satisfying. In 1969 I said to myself, "I think we can." Now, six years later, I look back and say, "I believe we did."

I'm sure all of you have your favorite memories of those six years. There were times when town government moved like a well-oiled mechanism, conquering all obstacles. And there were times when human error and honest differences of opinion made us look like we were just spinning our wheels.

In all that time, I can recall only a very few moments when I didn't totally enjoy being mayor of Chapel Hill.

In looking back over those years, I delight in the knowledge that this dynamic community has moved towards fulfillment of the basic campaign promises that I put forward in 1969.

I promised public transportation. And today we have a bus system that provides dependable, low-cost service conveniently available to 95 percent of our citizens.

I promised improved town-gown relations. I feel that channels of communications between the town and university, and the town and students, are more active than ever before. I see this not only in high-level discussions in the chancellor's and vice chancellor's office, I see it also in the faces of students and townspeople as they tap their feet to bluegrass music at the Apple Chill street fair.

I promised better access to the mayor. When I took the oath of office, there wasn't even a closet shelf at Town Hall for the mayor.

Now, we have an established tradition of a mayor's office with a part-time mayor and full-time mayor's assistant accessible daily to all citizens.

I promised to improve working conditions and wages for town employees. Employee wages and fringe benefits have improved over 200 percent. And, during my term in office, we have hired the town's first full-time directors of housing, planning, finance, and personnel.

I promised creative leadership and have pursued this goal by creating a Human Services Department, establishing a Housing Loan Trust Fund, and obtaining federal funds for neighborhood development, open space purchases, and public transportation.

You know that I haven't fulfilled these campaign promises alone. These are the achievements of hundreds of citizens who have served on committees and boards and taskforces. These are the works of conscientious town employees. And most especially, this progress has been made possible by the creative labors of a remarkable group of aldermen.

I have been fortunate to be the quarterback of a great team. There have been some disagreements while we were in the huddle. But when we went up to the scrimmage line, it was the aldermen who kept me from getting smeared or creamed.

I love being mayor of Chapel Hill and would love to continue. But there comes a time when a person realizes he should step aside and allow new ideas, new concepts, and new leadership to have their day. Therefore, I have decided not to seek reelection to a fourth term as mayor of Chapel Hill.

Because I love this community, and this office, I have high hopes for my successor. Your next mayor will find the job increasingly demanding, both physically and mentally.

In fact we are entering a period when we will need to consider having a full-time mayor.

I believe I am leaving for the new mayor a stable, progressive environment that will encourage continued progress. Also, challenging opportunities, which will demand sensitive, creative, courageous, and visionary leadership.

In the meantime, Howard N. Lee will not be a lame-duck mayor. These old wings will keep flapping until the day a new mayor is elected and sworn in. I will continue an active, responsible, and productive leadership role, moving toward an orderly transfer of responsibility to those leaders who will be elected in the fall.

I am grateful to this community for trusting me with this position of leadership. I have tried to respond to that trust with integrity, sincerity, honesty, and energetically.

Finally, thank you, journalists, for your interest and fairness reporting the news during my years of service.

The night of December 1, 1975, I passed the gavel to the newly elected mayor, James C. "Jimmy" Wallace. It had been six years since I had accepted the gavel from former mayor Roland "Sandy" McClamroch, but it seemed only a few days before. I walked away with a strong sense of pride, a great deal of satisfaction, and absolute confidence that I had left a solid foundation on which Chapel Hill could and would build a bright future.

15 The Campaign for Lieutenant Governor

In January 1976, after spending most of 1975 traveling around the state and testing the waters, I announced that I would seek the Democratic Party nomination for the office of lieutenant governor. I felt optimistic about my chances of success, but most pundits predicted that I would finish last, regardless of the number of candidates in the race.

Jimmy Green, speaker of the North Carolina House of Representatives, had indicated that he would run. There were many others who were making noise about running, but when the dust cleared there were only four additional candidates: George Miller from Camden County; Waverly Akins, chairman of the Wake County Commissioners; John Jordan, son of the former United States Senator B. Everett Jordan, out of Burlington in Alamance County; and Herbert Hyde, a moderate progressive legislator from Asheville.

It was a vigorous campaign, but with Jim Hunt running for governor it was hard to raise money. Fortunately for me, as the only black in the race, I was able to stay visible. Despite many who doubted I would survive the primary, I finished first among the contenders in August 1976, but unfortunately I did not have a majority of the votes. Jimmy Green, a staunch conservative, finished second and immediately called for a run-off. Although Green resented having to run against me, he realized he had to take me seriously.

Both Green and I ran aggressive and hard-hitting campaigns. I led in the polls through most of the campaign. I had the silent support of Jim Hunt, although he had to publicly proclaim his neutrality. I was delighted to have the support of Bert L. Bennett Jr., a strong Jim Hunt backer, and State Senator Ralph Scott, who publicly endorsed me. I am convinced the Hunt people gave me as much support as they possibly could without jeopardizing their own campaign.

About two weeks before the runoff, the Jimmy Green campaign took off the gloves and began playing dirty. Each day they used subtle racial appeals through advertisements and whisper campaigns. One such adver-tisement depicted black and white candidates standing beside each other with the caption "Unless the people come out and vote on September 14, the election will be decided by a relatively small segment of the popula-tion." This was a message to the white voters to not let blacks elect the next lieutenant governor. I tried to position myself as close to the Hunt platform as possible by adopting many of his proposals on education and economic development. I focused on uniting North Carolina as one strong state by using the theme "One North Carolina, United from East to West." In spite of all these efforts, I felt the momentum slipping away. Unfortunately, I was hit with a knockout punch two days before the election, when a Green campaign supporter began circulating the rumor that if I were elected lieu-tenant governor, blacks would hire an assassin to kill the governor, mak-ing me governor. At first I did not believe such a ridiculous rumor would gain traction, but unfortunately I was wrong. It not only gained traction, it roared across the state like a wildfire in dry grass. By this time, I was run-ning low on money and was having difficulty raising more money, which meant I could not finance last-minute ads on radio and television.

When voting day arrived, I realized I was in trouble and my only hope was for a heavy black voter turnout. That did not happen. We could not motivate blacks to go back to the polls. We were always lucky to get the black vote to the polls the first time, and getting a heavy black vote back to the polls a second time was darned near impossible. I knew we had more challenges to get our voters back to the polls than Green would because of voter lack of interest, having to take time off from work, not having trans-portation, and not being motivated to believe that the election of a person for lieutenant governor, whether black or white, was going to make any difference in their lives. More of our people went back than we expected, but we fell sixty thousand votes short of what we needed.

We dropped off about 60 percent the second time around. If we could have gotten the same votes in the second primary, I would have won. Jimmy Green had some strong political people who understood how to campaign and how to buy votes. So they bought a lot of the black votes. They also paid a lot of the blacks to stay at home in key areas. He used every tactic that could be used. To be honest, as I look back on it now, part of the problem was my naïveté. I was learning how to be a politician on the job, but I was learning in an unrealistic arena. I lost the second primary 48 percent to 52 percent.

When it was over, I thought how ironic it was that a state that had made such progress in race relations had once again let racism determine the outcome of a political campaign. Race had been used to defeat Dr. Frank Porter Graham in his U.S. Senate campaign in 1950, and in 1976 it had once again been used to defeat me.

Chapel Hill did not prepare me to go forth into the larger state arena and be an effective campaigner. I was not prepared for a campaign against a person like Jimmy Green. I had made assumptions that didn't make sense. I assumed there was no chance of convincing conservatives to vote for me because I equated conservatism with racism. So I didn't even bother to campaign among conservatives. Instead, I felt I had to rely on white liberals and blacks for support. Looking back, I see that was a mistake. I didn't realize it then, but I was painting myself into a corner with a no-win combination. I claimed I wanted to represent all the people, yet in my speeches my statements were contradictory. I went around saying things like, "We liberals and blacks must come together and form coalitions and make sure we are the ones in power. If we are in power, we can direct which way this state goes." Every time I made one of those speeches with the press in the audience, and each time such statements appeared in the newspaper, it further painted me in a liberal left-wing corner. As I have reflected on many of my words, I now understand why I was not considered seriously by the conservatives or even many moderates.

So those were naive mistakes that I made. However, I did learn from them. I learned that in the future I should never make an assumption based on labels alone. For instance, I should never assume that conservatism equates with racism or prejudice or discrimination. This was the greatest lesson that came out of that whole campaign for me. Because I was not elected lieutenant governor, I learned how to play hard-nosed, insider politics, which prepared me for the future. I was told that North Carolina Senate leaders were so afraid I might beat Jimmy Green that they drew up legislation to strip the power from the lieutenant governor and put it in the hands of the president pro tempore of the Senate. Because I did not win, Jimmy Green enjoyed the power of the office. However, that power was taken away later, when Jim Gardner, a Republican, became lieutenant governor in 1988.

After reflecting through the years, I am convinced that I would have been chewed up, spit out, and rendered helpless. It is possible I could have been such an ineffective lieutenant governor that any future political hope

Howard Lee and his father visit Jimmy Green headquarters to concede defeat in the 1976 campaign for lieutenant governor.

for me might have vanished. At the same time, I could not understand that, but looking back, I realize fate was turning me in a different direction from the one I had chosen. I was destined for better opportunities ahead.

When the dust cleared, I was faced with a huge campaign debt of over ninety thousand dollars. With the help of good friends like Walter Royal Davis, I was able to liquidate the entire debt within six months after the campaign ended.

16 Pioneer in a Governor's Cabinet

After losing the 1976 runoff election for lieutenant governor to Jimmy Green, I still wanted to be actively involved in the upcoming general election but was unsure what role I could play. Shortly thereafter, I met with Jim Hunt, the Democratic Party nominee for governor, to discuss how I might be involved in the November general election. While North Carolina had a long history of electing the Democratic nominee, the 1972 elections had swept into office the first Republican governor in seventy-nine years. Jim Holshouser, a relative unknown, had defeated the very popular Democratic nominee, Skipper Bowles. The governor's office was the one Democratic state office lost that year. Consequently, Jim Hunt was leaving no opportunity for that to happen again. We agreed that Democrats had to win the 1976 election and pledged to work hard to ensure his election as governor. To my surprise and delight, Hunt asked me to serve as first vice chairman of the party, which I gladly accepted.

We also discussed the possibility that I might be given serious consideration for a cabinet post after the election should he win. I realized this might be a tough decision for him because he would be the first in this state's history to appoint a black person to serve in a governor's cabinet. But if any governor was inclined to make that step, I knew that Jim Hunt had the courage and commitment and was in the best position to do it. On the other hand, I had built a strong reputation of being a rational person and had developed a positive image that made me a good candidate. Having run in campaigns for congress and lieutenant governor, I had also built up a broad base of supporters, which would be helpful to both Hunt's campaign and the Democratic ticket.

During the months leading up to the November 1976 election, I traveled the state campaigning for Jim Hunt and the Democratic Party ticket. I was part of a team responsible for making sure there was a very heavy black voter turnout on Election Day. This time there were no upsets. Jim Hunt and the entire Democratic ticket were elected by a comfortable margin.

Accepting the oath of office administered by Secretary of State Thad Eure.
Governor Hunt looks on.

In late November, Governor-elect Jim Hunt appointed me to the position of secretary of the Department of Natural and Economic Resources,
a department with a $350 million budget and 2,500 employees. Not in my
wildest dreams had I thought I would hold such a prestigious and responsible position of leadership and power. News reports noted that I was the
first black cabinet member in the South.

There were some who questioned Hunt's decision to select me as a cabinet
member. Of course, I felt I understood why he chose me. First, we shared
many of the same goals and commitments to ensuring a responsive government. Second, we both were publicly committed to attracting high-quality
industry to North Carolina and finding ways to place good jobs in rural
economically depressed communities. Third, we both believed we should
be accountable for protecting the state's environment while balancing environmental regulations with community development. Finally, we agreed
that education was a priority, and strong public schools were essential to
the future of North Carolina.

I voluntarily committed to Governor Hunt that I would put my own political ambitions on hold while serving as a member of his administration.

After I was sworn in, the governor and I worked closely to select the
best people for the positions of deputy secretary and the two positions of
assistant secretary. The governor chose Jack Smith, a Raleigh businessman,

Governor Jim Hunt with his cabinet members, 1977: (front row, Left to Right) Tom Bradshaw, Mark Lynch, Howard Lee, Sarah Morrow, Sarah Hodgkin, Burley B. Mitchell Jr., Amos Reed, Lauch Faircloth, Joe Grimsley; (back row, Left to Right) Governor Hunt and Secretary of State Thad Eure.

to be deputy secretary and named Eva Clayton of Warren County to an assistant secretary position, upon my recommendation. Eva was considered a real asset because of her ties to eastern and rural North Carolina. Eva had run for the second district congressional seat in 1968 and was a proven administrator and a very effective community organizer. This made her a natural for the position.

During the campaign, candidate Jim Hunt had promised to create a department to focus on meeting the needs of local governments. Therefore, my first challenge was to reorganize the department and transfer the economic development division to the Department of Commerce. I then replaced the economic development division with a new division to be known as the Division of Community Development. Governor Hunt wanted the department to become a "one-stop shop" for local government services. During the 1977 session, legislation was passed approving the reorganization and authorizing the name change to the Department of Natural Resources and Community Development (NRCD).

As the first black member of a governor's cabinet in North Carolina and the South, I did not want to be perceived solely as the black representative of the Hunt administration. During my days as mayor of Chapel Hill, I always resisted being drawn into the deep pit of racial representation. Yet there was enormous pressure from some black leaders who wanted me to become the spokesman for black communities throughout North Carolina.

Many blacks expected me to solve long-neglected and age-old problems overnight. For example, when there were racial problems in Wilmington and Greensboro, I was expected to become the mediator. I did not see this role as one I should be expected to play or one I wanted to play. I felt such engagement would be a diversion from my primary responsibility of overseeing a major state department. I declined to be drawn into that role, but the pressure never relented.

More than anything else, I saw my role as a trail blazer for young people, especially young blacks. I wanted to reach out and be a leader who could help bridge the gap between the diverse segments of the state. During my entire public career, I tried to serve all citizens without regard to race, socioeconomic status, or any other label.

As I settled into my role as department head, I was intrigued by the fishing industry. The more familiar I became with the history and challenges of this industry, the more I was drawn to finding ways to revitalize the fishing industry in the state. In spite of being warned that this was a very volatile area, I was not deterred and decided to push ahead.

After a few months and countless briefings, I directed that a meeting be arranged with the fishermen in Morehead City in order to open the channels of communication with this group. Several staff members did everything possible to convince me that it would not be smart to subject myself to what could be a very abusive meeting. They were really concerned that the fact I was black might not be welcomed by some of the fishermen. Even the governor's office and the governor himself had some concerns about me plunging into this water so soon. I almost allowed myself to be talked out of making the trip, but I felt I had no choice. I could stay in Raleigh and be afraid to tackle tough issues across the state or, if I was to be an effective secretary and serve the governor well, I had to be among the people. I knew the fishermen distrusted the state bureaucracy and that other secretaries had struggled to bridge the gap. Yet I felt the need to take on this challenge and was determined to succeed. I was confident I could deflect any racial feelings, but I was less sure I could deflect their mistrust of government.

I arrived at the meeting site and was met by Ed McCoy, the director of the marine fisheries division. He told me it seemed as if every fisherman on the coast had shown up for this meeting. I walked into the room in a three-piece suit with a white-on-white, French-cuffed shirt; no question I was overdressed. As the director and I walked slowly to the front of the room, I could feel the cold stares. The room was packed with commercial fishermen sitting stone-faced, with arms folded, and dressed in their work clothes. It was obvious some had come directly from their boats and brought the fish smell with them. I was told many had arrived early to see if I would actually show up and to hear what I had to say.

I decided I needed to dress down, and I did so quickly. While I was being introduced, I took off my coat, ripped off my tie, undid my cuff links, rolled up my shirtsleeves, and unbuttoned my shirt collar.

I began my speech by admitting that I had limited knowledge about the fishing industry but was eager to learn. I emphasized that I had spent hours, since Governor Hunt appointed me secretary, learning about the history of their relationship with the state. I told them I understood their frustration over feeling ignored, disappointed, and left swinging in the wind or floating on the water. I promised that at the direction, and with the support of, Governor Hunt, things would change, and change quickly. As I referenced points of obvious interest in my speech, I noticed that several unfolded their arms and others began to sit up straighter. I could tell they were actually listening. I continued, requesting they share with me their most pressing needs and what they wanted from the governor. I promised that whatever they shared with me I would share directly with the governor. Then I clinched it by saying I planned to hire a person who would be my full-time eyes and ears and who would be accessible to them twenty-four hours a day. After about twenty minutes, I stopped and said, "It's now your time to talk to me. I bet there have been times when you've said to yourselves, should I ever get a chance to talk with that governor or secretary, here's what I would tell both of them. That's exactly why I am here and what I want to hear."

During the next hour, they spilled their guts. It was clear they were angry because they felt many of their serious problems had not been solved. They talked about idle promises and false hopes that conditions would be improved and markets would be open, but this had never happened. They felt the folks in Raleigh created hope but dashed it when the state failed to complete the development of a seafood harbor called Wanchese. My staff took several pages of notes.

As the meeting was about to end, a fisherman stood and said, "I came here tonight to give you hell for all the false promises that have been made to us by Raleigh. I get the impression you might be an honest fellow. I don't know why, but I believe you are sincere." He then pledged his full support and said he really looked forward to working with me.

My closing statement was, "I will work with my staff to determine how we can make immediate efforts to start resolving many of these problems." I promised I would return to give them a full report of success or to face the music for not keeping my promise. After I thanked them for coming, I was surprised when they all stood up and started clapping.

As a result of this meeting, I was able to resolve some of their problems quickly. Within two weeks after the meeting, I appointed Joe McClees as my eastern North Carolina ombudsman. His job was to make sure we worked to solve the problems of the fishing industry and improve relations with the fishing community. I also appointed several working committees to search for ways to resolve the more difficult issues. After one year, I returned and found the fishermen in a more upbeat mood. I had not satisfied all their concerns, but had made enough progress that they were optimistic about the future of the industry. I met with them annually during my four-year term and enjoyed a long and productive relationship with the fishermen.

While I was determined to keep myself racially neutral, I did not hesitate to take on discrimination and prejudice when it raised its ugly head and when I felt it was within the context of my responsibilities as secretary.

One such incident occurred when I received a complaint that a private water company in the eastern part of the state was refusing to serve a small community of blacks. The company, which was requesting state grants for a project, had stopped its pipelines at an entrance to a black community, denying them access to water. When I asked why, the reasoning was "because the homeowners couldn't afford to pay." When I asked for confirmation, the company was unable to document the claim. The homeowners all confirmed that they were both able and willing to pay. After carefully investigating, my staff determined this was a blatant act of racial discrimination. On that basis, I informed the principals that unless people were served equally, both black and white, the company would not be awarded permission or granted a permit to serve anyone. Initially, the company balked and indicated it would appeal to the governor. I knew I was on solid ground and that Governor Hunt himself would not tolerate this type of behavior. After the governor's staff backed my position, the company quickly

Meeting with Ray Marshall, secretary of labor in the Jimmy Carter administration.

understood the error of its ways, and relented. The water line was extended to the black community.

The Wilmington Ten case in 1977 was one of the hottest and most racially divisive issues confronting the Hunt administration and the one that brought the greatest public wrath on my head. Nine black men and one white woman had been sentenced to a combined total of 282 years in prison after being convicted of arson and conspiracy following demonstrations in Wilmington in February 1971. They were still in prison when the CBS television news program *60 Minutes* ran a feature in early 1977 suggesting that all ten were innocent. Governor Hunt was under excruciating pressure to pardon or release the defendants. The issue was clearly divided along racial lines. Many moderate blacks and whites demanded that I urge Governor Hunt to pardon all ten defendants. Most whites, however, were adamant that no pardon should be granted. Even Governor Hunt's cabinet members had differing opinions.

At a meeting with a group of black leaders, I was reminded that my appointment was made possible by the large number of blacks who supported Jim Hunt and who had urged him to appoint a black cabinet member—specifically, me. I reluctantly agreed to speak to the governor. I met with the governor and several members of his staff for about an hour discussing the pros and cons of any action he might take. I made my case in favor of pardon. I was convinced the white community would be upset for a short time, but the black community would keep the flames fanned forever. I urged him to "pardon and put this behind us." Others made their counter arguments. I could sense that the governor was agonizing, both because of possible political ramifications and because of the seriousness of the charges. In a subsequent meeting, he shared that he had decided to commute the sentences of all except that of the Reverend Ben Chavis, the leader. He asked if I would stand with him. I said, "Governor, it would be easier on me if you were to pardon them all, but I can and will defend your decision." I concluded that gaining some reduction in the sentence would be an acceptable compromise.

I did not anticipate the wrath that I would endure from some within the black community. Some black leaders were upset that I supported the governor's actions and accused me of selling out. Some went so far as to demand that I publicly condemn the governor and resign my cabinet position in protest. While I understood their disappointment, I was not about to resign—cutting off my nose to spite my face. I received many threatening letters and some late-night threatening telephone calls and was publicly rebuked by some UNC black students. On the other hand, many moderate black leaders joined with me and stood in support of Governor Hunt's decision.

When I publicly refused to criticize Governor Hunt and announced I would not resign my position, the outrage intensified. In a speech shortly after the decision was released, I stated, "It would be unfair and unfortunate if Jim Hunt and his administration were judged solely on the Wilmington Ten episode."

I eventually felt the full force of the anger of a small group of blacks who demonstrated in front of McKimmon Center at North Carolina State University, Raleigh, where Governor Hunt was scheduled to speak at a human relations banquet. I arrived late with my wife and had to walk through a group of protesters assembled in front of the building. We were heckled, which was understandable. But then, without warning, a woman ran up and hit my wife Lillian in the back with a sign, almost knocking her to the ground. This was the first and only time I can recall publicly losing my cool. Acting on unconscious emotion, I started after the woman. Fortunately, a friend, Marion Rex Harris, grabbed me and held me back until I calmed down. We proceeded to the dinner while I was being called "Uncle Tom," "System Nigger," and "Oreo," among many other names. But I felt comfortable with my stance and saw no need to apologize; I was committed to continuing to serve with honor. Through the years since, as I have reflected on this incident, I felt I was right then and still do.

In January 1978, Governor Hunt made a televised speech outlining his intentions and indicating he would not pardon the Wilmington Ten. He did, however, reduce the sentences, as he indicated he would.

In December 1979, I was delighted when Governor Hunt called to tell me that he would be releasing Ben Chavis, the last of the Wilmington Ten remaining in prison. Shortly after his release, Chavis and I met face to face for the first time at a legislative Black Caucus event. He came to me, stuck out his hand, and we embraced. He then made a statement that both surprised me and gave me a feeling of vindication. He said, "No matter what people say about you, I think that you are a very good man. I have a lot of respect for you, and I respect the difficult positions you have had to take." Unlike many of his admirers, Ben understood that a black official had to tread carefully once in power and use his position of influence wisely. My respect for Ben Chavis went up after that encounter.

Another major accomplishment that still brings me pride was the establishment of the North Carolina Zoological Park. In spite of many early distractions, the governor wanted me to complete the first phase of the project by June 15, 1979. The park development had been floundering, and even though millions of dollars had already been invested there was little to show for the investment. Animals were being held in temporary houses and exhibited in primitive conditions. The governor directed me to lobby the legislature for the twelve million dollars needed to complete the first phase. Naively, I went to the General Assembly thinking this would be an easy task—and immediately hit a stone wall. It turned out that the legislature had appropriated one million dollars for the park years before and was told there would never be any further request for funding. The legislative leaders were therefore in no mood to consider a major additional request to build a zoo.

I eventually made my way to state Senator Russell Walker, who lived in Asheboro, the home of the zoo. Together we mobilized hundreds of zoo supporters, business leaders, environmentalists, schoolchildren, and citizens from all across North Carolina. Governor Hunt also used his influ-

Lee and Jim Fowler of the television show Animal Kingdom *touring the North Carolina Zoological Park on the eve of its official opening, June 1979.*

ence to keep the door open and persuade the legislature to appropriate the money. Appearing before several committees to outline how the money would be used, I related the zoo to educational and economic development enhancements in the state. During the last days of the legislative session, the prospects still looked dim. I thought we had failed, but somehow, at the eleventh hour, Senator Walker prevailed, and we were able to get the money into the budget.

The zoo project was elevated to the highest priority and the first phase, called Africa, was completed and officially opened by Governor Hunt in June 1979. Jim Fowler of the popular television show *Animal Kingdom* was invited, by me, to be the special guest at the opening. I was very proud to be a part of this historic achievement, making North Carolina the first state in the region to develop a natural animal habitat zoo.

At the end of my first two years as secretary of Natural Resources and Community Development (NRCD), I had enjoyed phenomenal success. I had successfully led the expansion of the Housing Finance Agency to help communities with development of affordable housing for moderate- and low-income citizens. I had also developed and implemented a plan to clean and rehabilitate polluted rivers across the state. One river that was made a top priority was the Chowan River in Pamlico County. This river, among the worst in the state, had been polluted over many years by toxic waste dumped from a nearby chemical plant. Environmentalists were pressuring us to take decisive action both to clean up the river and to sanction the parent company, Texas Gulf Sulfur. A series of meetings with the company resulted in agreements to cease dumping untreated toxins in the river. The company finally got the message that we were serious about reviving this river and would heap hefty fines on them if necessary. They began cooperating, and I launched the most massive cleanup effort the state had undertaken up to that time. I continued to lead the effort to implement the cleanup plan.

Recognizing the need to better protect natural resources in and around the North Carolina barrier islands and sounds, I successfully worked to strengthen the Coastal Area Management Program.

I also partnered with the federal government and several local governments to initiate the Mountain-to-Sea Trail. This is one of my proudest accomplishments. This trail allows hiking from the western North Carolina mountains to the seashores in eastern North Carolina. I am delighted this trail has continued to be improved and is one of the longest nature trails in the state.

In early 1978, after one year in office, I was feeling confident and comfortable in my role as cabinet secretary. It was then things started to go bad, really bad. The department internal auditors discovered signs of inappropriate handling of contracts within a federal jobs training program known as CETA (Comprehensive Employment and Training Administration). I was advised that I needed to take some drastic action, including possibly terminating some contracts and closing down the program. I finally made the decision to follow the staff's advice. Ultimately, criminal charges were brought against several individuals and some went to jail for stealing.

In the summer of 1978, I was hit with another crisis. Tanker trucks, owned and operated by Ward Transformer Sales and Service, Inc. of Durham, illegally sprayed a deadly chemical, polychlorinated biphenyl (PCB), on the shoulders of more than two hundred miles of state roadsides in fourteen North Carolina counties. The pollution was discovered when residents reported that something was causing their eyes to sting, their noses to burn, and many to feel sick to their stomach. The problem was traced to the oily brown toxic waste along the roads. When my staff received this report, I was urged to take immediate and aggressive action. I called the governor's office and spoke with his press secretary, who told me Governor Hunt was on vacation and shouldn't be disturbed unless there was a crisis. Because I didn't think this incident rose to that level, I decided not to bother him. I was told that as secretary of natural resources, it was my responsibility to handle such problems. On that basis, I assembled my staff and began mapping out a control and cleanup strategy.

But as word spread about the incident, the news media became curious and wanted a statement about our plans for cleanup and for apprehending and prosecuting the perpetrators responsible for dumping the toxins on the highway. I again consulted the governor's office about how to handle the news media and was told I should talk to the media but keep the governor's office informed. I held a news conference to discuss our response. I was very surprised by the number of reporters who showed up for the news conference. I was very forceful about how we would work with law enforcement to catch the culprit. I said, "Under no circumstance will we tolerate anybody contaminating our roadways, or the improper handling of toxic substances. I commit that we will do everything within our power to catch the perpetrators and prosecute them to the fullest extent of the law."

That night, as Governor Hunt watched the evening news, there I was, being broadcast all over the United States. I was shocked that this news conference was being broadcast nationally. It was then we all realized this problem was bigger than any of us had anticipated. Because it would require the involvement of several departments, it made more sense to coordinate the response out of Governor Hunt's office. My department continued to be a member of the team, but this was a much bigger problem than a single cabinet secretary could solve. The owner of the company was eventually arrested, tried, and sentenced.

Then the dominoes started to fall. In the summer of 1979, the department's internal auditor informed me that an Opportunities Industry Center (OIC) in Roper, North Carolina, was found to have serious bookkeeping problems. Upon further investigation he found some misappropriation of money and fraud. He recommend closing it down. After personally investigating, I felt the problem was with the director and not the program. The program had been successful and was providing badly needed services in an area of the state desperately in need. Eva Clayton, the assistant secretary, persuaded me it would be premature to close the program. She recommended that we replace the director instead. I agreed and directed that we keep funding the center but tighten our oversight. I also demanded that we launch a full-scale investigation and prosecute any person who had broken the law.

A few weeks after I had issued my directive, the *Raleigh News and Observer* newspaper was tipped off about the problem by someone from within the department. Pat Stith, a reporter, wrote a hard-hitting article highlighting all the negatives about the program at Roper, but did not report on the corrective action that had been taken. When Governor Hunt read the article, he decided to initiate an investigation out of his office. Because the program was under the auspices of the department of NRCD, it was felt a higher-level, independent investigation would be more believable. Eventually, three employees were indicted, including the former director. However, I was relieved when the governor determined the program was operating properly and should be continued.

My real challenge, however, was still to come. On the heels of the OIC problems in Roper, the internal auditors found problems in another politically sensitive organization. This time, it concerned a subsidiary of the North Carolina American Federation of Labor–Congress of Industrial Organizations (AFL-CIO), which had grossly misused funds. The subsidiary was running a training program, Precision Graphics, to train workers in the printing business, and it was funded under CETA, the same federal-state jobs program where funds had been misused the previous year at the Roper Center.

This time the state auditor's office, the office of the state attorney general, and federal prosecutors together launched full-scale investigations. Pat Stith, the *News and Observer* reporter, began writing articles on a daily basis. By this time I was convinced that somebody from within the department was leaking information to the press. The state auditor's report found that more than $130,800 had been misspent or stolen. All the information gathered by the state auditor and the department auditors was turned over to prosecutors. In 1981 two people were indicted and were sentenced to serve time. I eventually hired a new director for the CETA program and initiated several layers of checks and balances.

In my last two years in the Hunt cabinet, I was constantly fighting one crisis after another. I was being criticized as a weak leader who had lost control and was unable to manage. These multiple crises were starting to create a negative image for me. Disgruntled staff members became openly critical of my leadership. Throughout 1979 there were continuing reports about my failure as a cabinet member, which resulted in increased calls for my dismissal. Even some of the governor's staff started to weigh in and fan the flames. Some were sending signals that I would be out soon. However, Governor Hunt made it clear I would remain in my position until he said otherwise. In late September 1979, ten employees resigned in protest, citing my failure to stand up and push for stricter air pollution standards for power companies. I knew the governor wanted me to build good relations with environmentalists, but I also knew he wanted me to balance standards against responsible industrial growth. He recognized I was doing that and encouraged me to stay the course.

Many of my powerful friends who had watched me being attacked day after day in the newspaper and had listened to people in the General Assembly trash me decided to come to my aid. One such friend was the late Senator Ralph Scott, who had endorsed me in my campaign for lieutenant governor and was one of the most respected statesmen in North Carolina. Senator Scott wrote Governor Hunt, "I am glad to see you stand up for your cabinet official. I have the feeling that some are out to get him, and I hope you will give him all the help you can. Howard has a very difficult job, and I really believe his honesty and integrity are above reproach."

I appreciated and respected the governor for standing with me, in spite

The eve of Lee's departure from the Hunt administration. Governor Hunt presented the official portrait, which hangs in the building housing the department. Looking on is his wife, Lillian.

of all the negative publicity. He took a political risk. I, also, took a political risk because there were so many ways I could have been tripped up. I am confident that we survived because we stood shoulder to shoulder. Through the years, we had invested a great deal in each other. We had walked down too many roads together to do anything that would leave the other damaged. We had both grown in the political arena from our days as Young Democrats. We stuck together because of our long friendship, belief in each other's honesty, and deep respect for all we had achieved jointly through the years. Together we were writing history. I believe we hoped that someday future generations might understand, appreciate, and be inspired by the lives of two men who came from very different backgrounds, yet built a common trail that others might follow.

Jim Hunt entered the 1980 campaign a heavy favorite to be reelected governor, but the CETA scandals in my department became a central focus in that campaign. His Republican opponent, I. Beverly Lake Jr., had strong name recognition and was expected to be a strong challenger. Lake also had the backing of the Congressional Club, a campaign and fundraising organization associated with U.S. Senator Jesse Helms. Those factors alone were enough to give me concern that Lake would target me in that campaign in an effort to tarnish Governor Hunt. I committed myself fully to minimizing the political damage rising out of CETA. Once again my efforts were thwarted when, early in the campaign, a jury found the Roper Center director guilty of embezzling federal job-training funds. Candidate Lake pounced on this like a hawk on a Junebug.

He peppered the airways with advertisements accusing both the governor and me of using the CETA program to pay off political supporters. He tried to paint us as untrustworthy. I felt a lot of responsibility for allowing the CETA program to become a campaign issue and vowed to work harder than ever to help Governor Hunt get reelected.

I breathed a heavy sigh of relief when Governor Hunt won his 1980 reelection campaign by a comfortable margin. In the process, however, I was concerned that our relationship had been damaged. I frankly did not expect to be appointed to a second term in his cabinet. In mid-November 1980, Governor Hunt summoned me to a meeting the mansion. I was prepared to submit my resignation and leave the administration at the end of his first term. I was, therefore, surprised when he asked me to continue as a member of his cabinet. I was delighted and happily accepted.

When Governor Hunt announced the names of his second-term cabinet members, many were surprised that my name was among them. It had been rumored among insiders that I would not be reappointed. Almost immediately the pundits intensified their attacks.

In June 1981, barely six months into the second term, and after serious thought and deep reflection, I resigned my cabinet post effective July 31, 1981. The pressure had continued to build and was taking its toll on me. I did not know where I would go or what I would do next, but I was sure it was time for me to move on.

17 Balancing Politics and a Business

left the Hunt administration with my confidence weakened, feeling somewhat defeated and just burned out. Since 1969 I had lived under constant public scrutiny, which sometimes left me feeling like I was living in a fish bowl. Being the first black to pioneer in the political arena, I felt the need to be perfect and beyond reproach. I was often reminded that I was setting the standard and that my actions would either make it possible for others to have a chance, or cause them to be denied opportunities in the future. I realized I was also imposing this pressure on myself. I had worked hard to not screw up and cause the door of opportunity to slam in the face of future generations. But in mid-1981, I felt I needed to retreat and reassess my future, especially in politics.

On July 31, 1981, the day I left the Jim Hunt administration, I had no definite plans, no job prospects, and no idea how I would support my family. As I have reflected on that time, I realize how dumb it was not to have developed a safety net. Frankly, I thought I would have an easy time finding a position in private industry, at institutions of higher education, or in some other area of the public sector. Obviously, my ego played a trick on me, causing me to overestimate my value. I really thought I would be in high demand and that opportunities would fall like leaves at my feet. I thought, "It won't be a matter of what I would do, but rather picking from the litter." It wasn't long before I realized that many of the doors I expected to swing open were not going to open. The leaves I expected to fall had been blown away. I struggled to get serious responses from the people who were my friends. Unfortunately, I was left without any solid possibilities.

I called on two longtime friends, Terry Sanford, president of Duke University, and Bill Friday, president of the UNC system. Both made efforts to be helpful, but there were no immediate results. Terry arranged meetings with executives of several major corporations, which resulted only in my being pleasantly received and given encouraging assurances.

Eventually, out of desperation, I swallowed my pride and went to see Joe Pell, one of Governor Jim Hunt's chief advisors. I told Joe I was scraping the bottom of my financial barrel and needed the governor's help. I did not expect to return to state government, but I felt a word from the governor's office might open some doors. Joe, always a courteous man, promised to look into some possible options, talk with the governor, and get back in touch.

I realized that when I left the Hunt administration, I had forfeited most of the political currency I had earned through the years. I never did hear back from Joe Pell, and I was just too proud to ask again. I was slowly resigning myself to a position of feeling like the "odd man out." I had led the way among black politicians in many respects in the state, but the CETA controversy and other problems at NRCD had left me broken and tired. I had also lost standing among some black leaders, and they were keeping their distance. In addition, other new black political leaders had emerged, thus diminishing my status as the "blue-ribbon rooster in the barnyard." Many more blacks were being elected to various offices. Since, in 1981, there were no big elections on the horizon, I was just not in demand. I began to better understand the saying, "Friendship ends where politics begins."

In spite of my struggle, I still had too much pride to beg for a handout. I accepted the fact that all doors in the public sector were closed and I could write off any chance of landing a position in the private sector. Then I got an unexpected call from Terry Sanford, who had arranged for me to be interviewed for a position at the headquarters of ITT in New York. I was flown to New York, where I spent the day meeting and talking with high-level executives. I was not excited about moving to New York, but I was prepared to accept almost any position with a reasonable salary. But I was never faced with making that decision, as no job was ever offered. I was very relieved not to be faced with the dilemma of whether to leave North Carolina and move to New York.

Two weeks later, I received a call from Dr. John Hatch, a member of the UNC School of Public Health faculty and a member of the board of directors of the New World Foundation, also located in New York. He encouraged me to become a candidate for the position of president of a small private philanthropic organization. I submitted my resume and was invited by Hillary Clinton, chair of the board, for an interview. We met at the offices of the Children's Defense Fund in Washington, D.C. I felt the interview had gone well and that I had a good chance of being selected. But I was never offered the position; the board of directors decided to promote the foundation's vice-president. I was disappointed, but understood why the board made the decision.

For six months, Lillian and I struggled financially, but we were able to survive on her salary and our savings. In order to remain positive, I would recite the words of my grandfather, "Don't worry, because tomorrow will be better than today." I didn't know that for sure, but it sounded good and kept me hopeful.

Finally a small break came in mid-January 1982. John Turner, who in 1981 had become the first black dean of the UNC School of Social Work, called and offered me a part-time position to teach a class at North Carolina A&T State University in Greensboro. John and I had known each other for many years, having served together on boards of several national organizations while he was still dean at Case Western Reserve University in Cleveland, Ohio. I accepted, and began traveling between Chapel Hill and Greensboro once a week. The pay was not great, but I was able to supplement the income through independent lectures and speeches. I also gave a series of lectures at the University of Georgia School of Social Work. These were arranged by my old friend, Jim Shimkus, a former coworker in Savannah, former classmate at UNC, and now a University of Georgia faculty member.

In May of 1982, John Turner called to tell me that he and Bill Friday had discussed my situation and he was prepared to hire me as his executive assistant. My job would be to enhance and develop opportunities for the School of Social Work to become more involved with the broader community and community agencies. The salary was thirty thousand dollars a year, which was equal to my cabinet post salary. I started the new job in August 1982. This position helped greatly to restore my dignity and give me a feeling of security. In addition to the executive assistant duties, I continued to teach at A&T, with an additional class at UNC in Chapel Hill.

In October 1982, John invited me to collaborate with him and others to write and submit a proposal to the McConnell Clark Foundation, a small organization based in New York. To our delight, our proposal—to study ways to enhance struggling families and children living in poverty conditions—was funded in the amount of two million dollars. After the grant was awarded, John asked me join the project staff with an increase in salary to thirty-six thousand dollars. I felt great relief at having weathered the worst of the financial storm. I was starting to feel more optimistic about getting my life back on more solid financial footing.

By late 1983, I was starting to feel the itch to get back in the political arena. I was pondering the possibilities of making another run for the U.S. Congress. This thought was triggered when Ike Andrews, the incumbent Democratic congressman representing the fourth district, indicated that he might not run for reelection. I felt I would have a good chance of winning the seat. I talked with several key political leaders, including Jim Hunt and Terry Sanford, about running. I was encouraged to run if I was sure Andrews would not be running. While no one knew for sure, it was the collective wisdom that he would not run.

Based on that speculation, I spent January and February 1984 lining up supporters, identifying sources of campaign funds, and organizing the district. I felt really good about the level of support being pledged, although most of it was contingent on the congressman not running. Based on what I knew, at the time, I was sure he would not run.

But in early March, Andrews announced that he would be filing to run for reelection. I was thrown for a loop. I met with several of my supporters and staff to determine what to do. I started getting calls from friends and supporters indicating that running against Andrews would be a bad move. Many pledged to support me contingent on his not running, but they felt obligated to support him. I felt like I was sitting on a tree limb and watching it being slowly sawed off.

A wise man would have thrown in the towel, folded the tent, and backed away. But I wasn't inclined to act wisely or logically. I needed a way back into the political arena and felt this was my time. I felt compelled to push forward because polling indicated that Andrews was vulnerable. I calculated that the worst-case scenario for me would be a narrow defeat. So, in March 1984, in spite of all the discouraging signs, I filed and became an official candidate.

I was feeling good about my decision, but two weeks after filing, there was an unexpected development. The son of John Winters Sr., a prominent black leader in Raleigh, also filed as a candidate. John Winters Jr. had never held a public office and had never been a candidate. It was obvious that he had been persuaded to enter the race in order to split the black vote. I knew that with a substantial portion of my vote base diminished it would be difficult for me to win the primary election. Nevertheless, I ran what I felt was a hard and effective campaign and believed I was in a strong position to win. On election night, I had an early lead based on the votes from Orange County and some of the predominantly black precincts in Durham. But when the Wake County votes were reported, the tide shifted. The race was still too close to call as the last precincts reported. But as the final precincts reported in from Wake County, the outcome was exactly as expected. Ike Andrews won the primary, with slightly over 50 percent of the vote.

After I lost the primary, I worked hard to help get Andrews elected in November. In spite of all our gallant efforts, he lost to Bill Cobey, a Republican and former UNC athletic director. I was disappointed that I had lost the primary election and equally disappointed that Andrews lost a solid Democratic seat to a Republican. The experience of this campaign left me with a bitter taste in my mouth, mainly because John Winters was more of a spoiler than a serious candidate. His campaign siphoned off votes from my campaign. I decided then to pursue other interests and become a business owner.

In late 1985, when American Airlines announced plans to establish a hub operation at the Raleigh-Durham Airport, I submitted a bid to provide concessions stores for the new terminal. I contacted American Airlines and was invited to a meeting in Dallas, Texas. When I arrived at the American Airlines headquarters with my proposal, I was told that the concessions had been awarded to American's subsidiary, Sky Chef Caterers. However, I was encouraged to contact Sky Chef to determine what opportunities, if any, would be available to form a partnership as a minority-owned company. I walked over to the Sky Chef headquarters, located in an adjacent building and was able to arrange an appointment for the next morning.

The Sky Chef representatives were so impressed with my proposal and financing that I was offered space for two stores: a specialty foods concession, selling Famous Amos cookies, Häagen-Dazs ice cream, and natural snacks; and another, a bakery. I was more than happy with the offer, eagerly accepted, signed documents of intent, and returned home to complete my planning. I realized this agreement would have to be approved by the Raleigh-Durham Airport Authority, but because I had a good relationship with the staff and several Authority members I didn't perceive that to be a problem. But two days later, I was whiplashed. Dobbs House, which catered most southern airports, filed suit to protect its fifty-year monopoly rights for food concessions at Raleigh-Durham Airport. Sky Chef and American decided not to fight. I lost my deal with the bakery, but still had the specialty foods concession.

I immediately contacted Dobbs House and negotiated a partnership agreement to open and operate a bakery. I financed my company, Lee Airport Concessions, with a combination of loans and lines of credit from several financial institutions totaling nearly a million dollars.

Everything was progressing well toward the date when the new terminal would open, June 15, 1987. But disaster struck one week before I was to open. Sky Chef sold its terminal concession operations to another company, and although I was able to keep the stores at the airport, I lost the right to sell the Häagen-Dazs ice cream and Famous Amos cookies brands. I had a freezer packed with Häagen-Dazs ice cream and Famous Amos cookie dough and was instructed to return both products to the distributor. Overnight, I was out of business before I ever opened. I had to scramble to find another source of ice cream and cookies or I would have a store with no products to sell. I asked Sky Chef to intervene, but was told I had to make my own arrangements. It was clear that Sky Chef and the Airport Authority expected me to be ready to open on June 15, with both cookies and ice cream. Sky Chef did, however, give me the name of a cookie company in New York. I was able to negotiate agreements with David's Cookies for cookie dough and Pine State Creamery of Raleigh for ice cream. When the first plane landed on June 15, Lee Airport Concessions opened the cookie and ice cream store. And two weeks later, I opened the bakery, under the name of Vie de France, a French bakery.

I was involved in the day-to-day management of the business, working sixteen hours a day. In 1990, I found myself back in politics and needed to make different arrangements for managing my business. Fortunately, I was able to put a plan in place for Sky Chef to manage the specialty foods store and for Dobbs House to manage the bakery. This freed me to concentrate on my duties in the senate. This arrangement worked well until March 1994, when the Airport Authority rescinded their permission to allow me to be an off-site owner. I was given three choices: sell the stores, hire an on-site manager, or personally assume day-to-day control by July 1, 1994. This directive could not have come at a worse time. I was in the middle of organizing my campaign for reelection to the state Senate. Therefore, between July and November, I had to balance managing my business at the airport and running for reelection. As it turned out, I lost the general election to my Republican challenger, Teena Little. I spent the next six months managing my business full-time.

In September 1995, however, I hired a full-time manager with more than fifteen years of experience in the airport concessions business. This arrangement gave me more flexibility to pursue my political interests. Shortly after this, in January 1996, I decided I would once again seek reelection to the N.C. Senate, and this time I was successful.

In 2000 the Airport Authority granted us a ten-year franchise and approved plans for nine stores to be built over two years. By 2001 we had opened six stores and had three more planned for construction. I had a workforce of more than seventy employees and was in the process of evaluating several other regional airports. My company was experiencing its most profitable year ever, with gross income at an all-time high.

Then disaster hit. It was September 11, 2001, when the New York World Trade Center buildings collapsed after being rammed by two hijacked passenger jets. Air travel was paralyzed, and those of us in airport concessions throughout the United States were ordered to lock our doors and vacate the airport terminals. By the end of that day, my business was shut down. I was not able to reopen for two weeks, and by then my business was in shambles. I had to open in stages and reduce my workforce to thirty people. My company was financially strained, and my personal assets were being drained. I eventually had to sell a major interest in my business in order to keep the operation afloat. Though I did everything possible I was never able to return it to profitability. I was forced to release my manager in 2004 and transfer the day-to-day management to my minority investor. Then in December 2005, I decided to throw in the towel. After fourteen years in the airport concessions business, I sold the balance of my interest and walked away. I was fortunate to be able to pay off all my debt. I never realized the great personal financial windfall that had been on the horizon before the September 11 disaster.

Despite these upsets, I look back now and cherish the experience of being in the airport concessions business.

18 North Carolina State Senator

During my years in business, the dream of once again holding a public office was never too far from my thoughts. To my surprise, that opportunity came in the fall of 1989 when Senator Wanda Hunt unexpectedly resigned. Like an addict, I could not resist the temptation to jump in and compete to fill the vacant seat. I immediately served notice that I would be seeking the Democratic Party appointment to serve out the remainder of her unexpired term. However, it turned out to be a tougher challenge than I had anticipated. The first barrier was to convince the Democratic women not to demand that a woman replace Senator Hunt and to instead support me. The selection was to be made by Democratic Party representatives from the four county districts of Orange, Chatham, Moore, and Randolph. Ultimately, I and two women applied for the seat. Margaret Pollard, a Chatham County resident, was the most formidable candidate; by the time she announced her candidacy, she had already locked up the two votes from Chatham. The two women who represented Orange County's two votes, which I thought would automatically accrue to me, also decided to support Margaret. In spite of my efforts to diminish the gender factor, they decided that the replacement should be a woman and should be a resident of Chatham County.

I knew this could mean big trouble. In order to win, I needed all of the votes from both Moore and Randolph counties. I had campaigned hard for the votes from Moore County, which paid off when both Moore delegates decided to commit to me. One of the two delegates from Randolph County committed to support me, but the second remained undecided. This one vote mattered, since it would decide the winner. Eventually, Russell Walker, a veteran state senator and longtime friend from Randolph County, used his influence and persuaded the second Randolph County delegate to vote for me. After more than two hours of deliberation, I was chosen on the first ballot. I felt it was ironic that the Democratic delegates from two

Republican-dominated counties secured my victory. This would be the only time I would win majority support in either of these two counties.

In January 1990, I was sworn in to complete the one remaining year of Wanda Hunt's unexpired term. Immediately after being sworn in, I met with the Senate president pro tempore, Henson Barnes. I had enjoyed a very good relationship with Henson during my days as secretary of the Department of Natural Resources and Community Development, when we worked together to expand the North Carolina Parks System. Consequently, he asked me to serve on several major committees. Some of the more senior members complained that I was being given special treatment and needed to pay my dues before being awarded special committee assignments. There is no question that Senator Barnes allowed me to be a part of his inner circle of advisors and accelerated my rise to the ranks of Senate leadership. Answering the critics, a senior member of the Senate, Kenneth Royal, said one day, "Howard Lee is not a freshman, he's a transfer student." I was especially pleased to be appointed to a Senate Committee on Appropriations and allowed to sit in on budget negotiations during the 1990 session.

However, to stay in office, I had to run and be elected to a full term in the November 1990 election. Fortunately, I had no primary opposition, but I did have a tough Republican challenge in the general election. Because this was a two-seat district, Russell Walker and I ran as a team on the Democratic ticket. We ran against two very strong Republicans. Fortunately, we won with a majority of the vote, and I began serving my first full term in the 1991 session of the General Assembly. This time Senator Barnes appointed me to serve on such prestigious committees as Education, Environment, Transportation, Finance, and Appropriations.

In 1991, I introduced several major pieces of legislation, but one became very controversial. A group of students from UNC Chapel Hill persuaded me to introduce legislation to repeal North Carolina's corporal punishment law. This law had been in effect for over a hundred years and required every public school to adopt a corporal punishment policy. I was unprepared for the firestorm that was created. I was surprised that many of my close political allies, such as the late Herbert Hyde and Dennis Winner, both from Asheville, N.C., were adamantly opposed. I eventually had to give up the effort to repeal the law and had to accept legislation that granted local school systems the option of forbidding the use of corporal punishment in their schools. This weaker bill eventually passed the house by a few votes and was enacted by the Senate by one vote.

The legislation of which I am most proud extended budget management flexibility to the state university system. Before this legislation, universities had to spend appropriated funds only in the lines assigned or return the money to the general fund. The debate on this bill was long and protracted in both houses. In spite of having the support of the leaders of both houses, there was concern that it would not pass a floor vote. It was during this experience that I began learning how to maneuver in the legislature. After several compromises, instead of bringing the bill to an up or down floor vote, it was included in the budget as a special provision. This was truly a crowning achievement for me. I was pleased to be the primary sponsor of legislation awarding the first-ever budget flexibility to the university system.

Near the end of the 1991 session, Senator Barnes announced that he would not run for reelection to the state Senate but would instead become a candidate for the office of attorney general. Once this news became public, several senators began jockeying for position to run for the coveted office of president pro tempore. In 1992 R. C. Soles from Columbus County, one of longest serving senators, announced his intentions to seek the office. I initially pledged my support to him, thinking he would not be challenged. A few weeks later, however, another senator, Marc Basnight from Dare County, indicated he would be a candidate and asked me to support him. This presented a very special problem for me. I had known Marc since my days as secretary of NRCD, when we worked together on projects to expand and enhance the fishing industry. I decided to test the water and determine whether Marc had a chance of winning. After all, he had been in the Senate for only eight years, having been elected in 1984. He had, however, served as chairman of the powerful Appropriations Committee, which positioned him well to attract support. He also had a very good personal friend of mine, Walter R. Davis, supporting him. Walter convinced me that Marc would be a strong leader for the Senate. Based on Walter's support and my deep respect for Marc, I was strongly inclined to become a part of the Basnight team. Marc indicated that my support would be a big boost to his chances. Once I determined he could win the position, I decided it would be in my best interest to support him. However, having committed my vote to R. C. Soles, I felt obligated to keep my word unless he released me. Initially, when I broached the subject of release, he was reluctant. But eventually he determined he would not have enough votes to win and decided to withdraw his candidacy. That freed me to join forces with Marc Basnight and help him organize a very effective campaign to become the next president pro tempore. On the opening day of the 1993 legislative session, Marc Basnight was unanimously elected president pro tempore of the N.C. Senate.

As one of the senators who actively supported Marc early on, I became one of his closest confidants and allies. Marc appointed me to both the Appropriations and Finance Committees. I was also appointed chairman of two other committees: Transportation Appropriations and Transportation Oversight. In my role as chairman of the Transportation Committee, I designed the plan that resulted in the initial funding for the Triangle Transit Authority. I also initiated one of the first studies on the value of toll roads for North Carolina. I was enjoying phenomenal success and had moved into a strong and powerful position in the Senate. At the end of the 1993 session, I was rated the eighteenth most effective senator out of the fifty in the Senate.

I ended the session on a high note and felt confident I would be reelected. I did not have a primary election, but was facing a tough Republican challenger again. Teena Little, a moderate Republican living in Southern Pines, decided to run for the Senate seat. Because the district was dominated by Democrats, I did not take her candidacy too seriously and was confident I would win hands down. Unfortunately, I miscalculated the impact of the Republican Party's national "Contract with America" campaign and a low vote turnout by Democrats. I got one of the biggest shocks of my life when the votes were counted and I had lost the campaign by eighteen hundred votes and was out of the Senate. For days after the campaign, I felt as if I was living a bad dream. The toughest challenge for me was cleaning out my office and leaving Raleigh. My first inclination was to throw in the towel and forget trying to serve in an elected office again, but I'd felt this way before.

Although I had enjoyed the airport concessions business, I still missed being in the Senate. Therefore, in late 1995 I started to think about organizing and launching a campaign to regain my seat. In January 1996, with my business under solid management, I announced my candidacy.

Unlike the two previous campaigns, this time I had to compete in a tough Democratic primary against two other candidates, Eleanor Kinnaird and Fred Hobbs, for one of the two seats. Surprisingly, I won the primary by more than three thousand votes, with Ellie Kinnaird placing second. In the general election, I had to face the Republican incumbent Senator Teena Little again. This time I was able to win by eighteen hundred votes—the same total I had lost by in 1994. I was elected to serve along with Ellie Kinnaird. I was absolutely thrilled to win and to be returning to the Senate. In January 1997, I was once again sworn in as a member of that body.

I was pleasantly surprised when Marc asked me to accept an appointment to serve as cochairman, along with Senator Leslie Winner, of the Senate subcommittees on education policy and appropriations. I considered this a fantastic opportunity. I was especially pleased to have the privilege of working again with Governor Jim Hunt, who was two years into his fourth term as governor. Governor Hunt was pushing hard to raise standards for public school students, increase salaries and standards for teachers, and increase appropriations for K-12 education programs. As Senate education leader, it was part of my responsibility to manage Governor Hunt's education reform legislation, called the Excellent Schools Act. This is now heralded as one of Governor Hunt's landmark legislative achievements. I also was a major sponsor of legislation establishing the Smart Start program, designed to serve preschool at-risk students. This was North Carolina's first major push to expand preschool. I was delighted to join with Governor Hunt and work hard for its passage and funding. Between 1997 and 2000, I managed all the education reform legislation enacted by the Senate and ultimately the General Assembly. I was the major sponsor of legislation on standards and accountability, safe schools, and improving low-performing schools.

I was reelected in 2000 without primary opposition and had only token opposition in the general election in November. When I took office in 2001, Marc appointed me cochairman of the powerful Senate Committee on Appropriations, along with Senators Aaron Plyler and Fountain Odom.

When Governor Hunt left office in 2001, he had positioned the state to prepare students to be successful in the twenty-first century. He wrote a book in which he challenged the state to build a strong education system that would be "First in America" by 2012. When Governor Mike Easley took office in January 2001, he committed to accelerating the goal of First in America, but his challenge was much greater. He wanted to emphasize preparing students to compete in a twenty-first-century economy. His new challenge was for North Carolina to be among the top educational systems in the world. Therefore, one of his first priorities was to enhance the learning experiences of four-year-olds. He proposed a new initiative called More at Four. When his request was introduced in the General Assembly, he found the budget was very tight and the legislature was resistant to funding any new programs. There was no line of legislators ready and eager to introduce and manage his education legislative proposals, especially the early childhood initiative More at Four. Because I was the chairman of the Senate Appropriations Committee, Governor Easley asked if I would introduce and manage his education agenda. As I anticipated, More at Four was a tough sell. I had to overcome resistance among both senators and representatives, as well as some token opposition from some Democratic legislators. I expected Republican legislators to be strongly opposed and to paint the proposal as just another Democratic spending program. I was not disappointed —but I was well prepared to beat back their opposition. Ultimately, we prevailed, and the More at Four program was enacted and funded with support from both Democrats and a few Republicans. This program has since become a major part of our progress in the North Carolina education reform process.

After the 2001 session, I was rated among the top five most effective senators and felt confident I would be reelected. Then disaster struck again. I found myself in the middle of another redistricting controversy. In 1972, as a legislative outsider, I had been denied the opportunity to run for Congress because of redistricting. In 2002, although I didn't know it at the time, I was about to be denied reelection to my state Senate seat because of redistricting. As a member of the Senate insider group, this time I played a major role in drawing district lines. Obviously, I tried to make sure my district was secure. Unfortunately, lawsuits were filed, and the courts rejected our initial district plan plus three subsequent plans. Republicans had filed the suits, demanding only single-seat districts, whereas we had been drawing a mixture of one-seat and two-seat districts. The Republican-dominated state supreme court agreed and directed the legislature to draw all single-seat districts. This meant that all two-seat district incumbents had to run against each other in a Democratic primary. Ellie Kinnaird and I were forced to compete against each other for the single seat in our district. We both were uncomfortable about the circumstance, but had no choice. I knew it would be a tough campaign, but I thought I could win. We both ran aggressive campaigns. When the election was over, I lost by just 114 votes.

One of my last pieces of education legislation that passed in 2002, after I lost the primary, was Job Sharing for Teachers. This teacher job sharing legislation was an effort to provide another option to keep teachers from leaving the classroom by allowing them to work part time. The legislation passed with overwhelming support in both the House and Senate. I remember presenting the bill in the North Carolina House of Representatives Education Committee which was unanimously given a favorable report. At the end of my presentation it was highlighted that this was my last appearance as a legislator before any committee. I was both surprised and flattered to be given a standing ovation by committee members. It was not customary that members of one legislative chamber would show such appreciation for a member of the other. The committee chairman indicated they wanted to thank me for all my hard work on education issues while a North Carolina Senator. My final session was both exhilarating and sad.

In December 2002, I cleaned out my Senate office and left the legislative building for the last time. It was much harder and more disappointing in 2002 than it was in 1994. I had taken the election very seriously and had campaigned very hard, but still I lost. I was a part of the power grid in the Senate, yet I was rejected. I was ranked among the top five senators out of fifty, yet that was not good enough to get me reelected. I found comfort in the fact that I had been a good senator who accomplished a great deal, enjoyed tremendous success, and made a lot of difference. I also knew I would remain politically active, although I didn't know what the future would bring. I did not have to wait long. Early in 2003, I visited Governor Mike Easley to discuss possible options for my future.

19 Educational Leader: Chairman of State Board of Education

To the best of my knowledge, no North Carolina governor had ever had a senior education budget advisor. But that's what I became in February 2003 for Governor Mike Easley. After meeting with Governor Easley, he decided that because I was highly respected among legislators of both political parties, I would be very helpful managing many of his education legislative initiatives.

Sometimes it feels strange to realize that I was in the Senate when Governor Jim Hunt needed a legislative leader to manage his initiative for higher standards in North Carolina's public schools. I felt even more fortunate to be in the Senate when Governor Easley needed a champion to push through his legislation establishing More at Four, the first-ever program for educating four-year-olds. I considered it an honor to be able to partner with Governor Easley as he pioneered this groundbreaking educational initiative for North Carolina. I considered it a special privilege to serve in the capacity of senior education budget advisor to the governor.

After only two months working with Governor Easley, he asked me to fill an unexpired term on the North Carolina State Board of Education and accept the position of chairman. I was delighted, and on May 1, 2003, with Governor Easley's blessings, I was unanimously elected by the board members and immediately took the oath of office.

Governor Easley wanted me to focus the board's attention on improving poorly performing schools, raising the level of respect for public education, and ensuring that every child in North Carolina had access to a sound basic education. My entire life seemed to have been preparing me for this role. Looking back, I believe I was destined to leave the North Carolina Senate because I was needed more to lead North Carolina's battle to improve and enhance public education.

Accepting the chairmanship of the State Board turned out to be one of the biggest and most exciting challenges in my public life. In the late nineties, the legislature decided that the Department of Public Instruction was an oversized bureaucracy. From 1995 to 1999, they proceeded with a massive downsizing from fourteen hundred employees to fewer than four hundred. By the time I arrived as chairman, the State Board and department were struggling to regain their position of respectability both among legislators and educational leaders throughout the state. Many local school superintendents were complaining about the lack of support and responsiveness from the department. They were not happy with the process used by the State Board to establish policies that impacted them, without their input. I accepted the challenge to work closely with the state superintendent, Dr. Mike Ward, to regain the confidence of the local leaders and the legislators. State Board members were urged to make special efforts to increase their visibility in their districts, spending time visiting schools and listening to concerns of educators and citizens.

While the legislature continued to reduce personnel in the Department of Public Instruction, it also continued to overburden the department with greater demands. Meanwhile, the department was losing many of its top professionals to local school systems, which offered better salaries and benefits. The governor challenged me to work to rebuild the department's reputation and strengthen the responsiveness of both the State Board and the department to the public.

In order to turn the ship around, I became an active chairman, dedicating more than 60 percent of my time to departmental and board activities. In the Education Building, I established the first-ever office for the board chairman. I traveled the state, meeting with superintendents and local school boards to rebuild relationships that had eroded. I spent a great deal of time working with legislative leaders to develop trust and reassure my friends and former colleagues that I was committed to providing the educational leadership the state needed from the chairman of the State Board. I considered myself the policy leader on behalf of the State Board and avoided inserting myself in the day-to-day operations of the department.

One of the major issues that confronted me as chairman was a ruling by state Superior Court Judge Howard E. Manning, who was presiding over the Leandro lawsuit. This lawsuit began in 1994 as an attempt to secure additional funding for poor school systems. About the time I arrived, Judge Manning issued directives to the State Board and Superintendent of Public Instruction requiring us to focus efforts and resources on improving seventeen of the lowest performing high schools in North Carolina. The judge targeted high schools scoring below 50 percent proficiency. Our challenge was to develop specific interventions for these schools to improve student performance. Governor Easley raised the bar even higher. He directed me, as chairman, to intervene and raise the performance of these schools above 70 percent proficiency. The State Board and I, as its chairman, accepted these challenges. We are making progress towards achieving better outcomes in these schools. I am happy to be the man at the helm, leading and overseeing the implementation of our plans.

I was well into my third year as chairman when on March 30, 2006, North Carolina launched its Education Lottery, established by the North Carolina General Assembly. As chairman of the North Carolina State Board of Education, I was given the honor of buying the first ticket sold in the state. The ticket is permanently displayed in the North Carolina Museum of History along with a picture of me purchasing the ticket. At the time, I purchased a total of five one-dollar tickets, one of which won ten dollars, doubling my investment. I contributed the ten dollars to the Early Childhood Education Fund.

As I reflect on this occasion, I consider it quite an ironic turn of events, remembering my open support of the lottery during my last campaign for the state Senate. This position may have been a major reason I lost in the 2002 Senate election. During the time I served in the North Carolina Senate, I had always favored the lottery. My position did not always reflect the attitude of many of my constituents in my senatorial district, as I found out during my 2002 campaign for reelection. My first challenge came during a campaign appearance at a retirement complex alongside my opponent for the Senate seat, plus candidates for the State House of Representatives. Each of us was asked to state our position on whether the legislature should allow a state lottery. The other three participants indicated they would vote no on any legislation presented. I felt like the odd man out. I had the choice of agreeing with my colleagues, which would have been a lie, or telling the truth and accepting the consequences. I indicated I would vote to support the lottery. After the event, several approached me indicating that if I did not change my position they would cast their vote for the other candidate. This scene repeated itself many times over throughout the district, but especially in the Chapel Hill area.

Many of my friends advised me to soften my stand and hedge my position. If I had taken their advice, it would have been out of character for me. I have always believed in presenting myself so the voters would have a clear understanding of my position on issues. I believe it is the responsibility of a candidate to state positions clearly and let voters make their decision.

Every campaign I have run was on that basis. I was not about to pull a bait-and-switch during the 2002 campaign for the Senate. Win, lose, or draw, I will always present myself as honestly and straightforwardly as possible.

I supported the lottery because I believed it would add millions of dollars to the state's coffers to fund educational programs, dollars otherwise being lost to the surrounding states. I have always thought that most people need something to dream about. Sometimes they need something to give them hope and a reason to believe that tomorrow will be better than today. It may never happen, and for most it does not, but the hope keeps people going, expecting to find the gold ring around the next corner. My life when I was growing up, and the lives of members of my extended family, were built on daring to dream and taking chances. My only paternal aunt, Nevada Lee, loved to "play the numbers" back in Lithonia. (Playing the numbers involved an illegal lottery where persons would bet on the volume of stocks and bonds traded every day on the New York Stock Exchange. The process disappeared with the advent of legal lotteries.)

Every day my aunt would bet a nickel or a dime on the numbers. She knew she probably would never win big, and she never did. But every morning she had a reason to get out of bed and check the newspaper to see if she had the winning numbers. Every once in a while she would win a few dollars and be very, very happy. It is true that she never got ahead. She understood what most people who play the lottery understand. While most intelligent people know it's a bad bet, for some it may be their only hope.

In 2005 Governor Easley asked me to fill a vacant seat on the N.C. Utilities Commission. I considered this to be a unique opportunity to serve the people of the state in yet another challenging role. I agreed to continue in my role as chairman of the State Board of Education, and I have found that the two roles complement each other. The legislature confirmed my appointment quickly, and I was sworn into office on April 1.

I have been associated with North Carolina governors since 1968 and feel blessed to have had that privilege. Governor Easley's administration built on the state's rich history and provided new programs in the educational arena. While North Carolina's public schools face tough challenges, I am optimistic about the future and believe there are brighter days ahead.

20 Looking Back, Looking Forward

As I have grown older, I have developed a deep appreciation for my southern experience and roots. My life, like that of most blacks from the 1940 to 1960 era, was subject to uncertainty and constant threats from segregationists and Klan oppressors. As I reflect on that time in my life, I am certain the experience prepared me for the hard knocks, disappointments, and challenges I have faced through the years. I learned how to get back up after being knocked to my knees and licking my wounds for a while, and then, how to jump up and get back into the ring of life and fight to survive. The words from the book of motivational quotes given to me by my mother described it in a more precise way: "I'm a little wounded but I am not slain, I shall lay me down for to bleed a while, then I'll rise and fight with you again." That's what growing up in the South taught me. I also developed a tough skin, along with a cautious attitude. I occasionally dreamed of how much easier life might be if things were different, if I was not black. Of course, when I awaken from such dreams and return to reality, I am satisfied with who I am. From my position in life today, I look back and rejoice that I could not make those boyhood dreams come true. In my adult life, I have transformed some of those dreams into an even better reality. I was once asked by a friend, "Howard Lee, if you could redesign your life and the circumstances in which you grew up, what changes would you make?" My response was and will always be—as I look back on my life's journey, I wouldn't change anything. I would still choose to be born black. I would still choose to be born in the South. I would still choose to be born to poor, struggling parents. I would live with my grandparents on the sharecropper's farm where I experienced profound happiness and joy like I had never experienced.

I am firmly convinced that my life was designed by a master creator for a special purpose. It is my sincere hope that I have come close to fulfilling my purpose. I consider many of my achievements to be minor miracles. In spite of everything, I am satisfied with who I am, who I have become, and all my accomplishments. I feel blessed to have survived the treacherous circumstances of my early years with dignity and to have done it my own way.

Growing up in the South and experiencing oppression and repression, it would have been so easy for me to hate the South. Instead, I grew up experiencing a love-hate relationship with the region. I never really wanted to leave, but felt I had no choice but to stay.

There have been times when I felt I was an apologist for the South because I enjoyed listening to and humming the song "Dixie," but didn't dare admit it. To me "Dixie" represented an expression of appreciation for the intrinsic beauty of the South and a strong feeling of pride and loyalty, rather than just the ugliness the region symbolized. Regardless of that ugly part of southern history, Adam Clayton Powell once commented that the South was, in some ways, more caring than the North. In his words, "In the South people are rejected as a race, but accepted as an individual. In the North, people are accepted as a race, but rejected as an individual." That is the South in which I lived and grew up and where I can now proclaim myself proudly as a loyal Southerner.

Conditions have changed now, and I am still living in the South. If I choose I can now sing "Dixie" without apology, although I expect many of my friends would still give me questionable looks and some, I am sure, would not find it amusing.

My days in Dixie were not all bad and certainly not all ugly. I have many fond and pleasant memories. I remember my days on the farm with my parents and grandparents who showed me comfort and assured me of my safety. I remember the love and warmth of family and their hopefulness of things to come and their belief in better days ahead. I remember the spacious fields of corn and cotton, the rows of watermelons and peanuts, the majestic magnolia trees that stood in our yard, the flowers that bloomed in spring, and the warm and comfortable temperatures in summer. That's what my mind's eye sees when I hear the tune "Dixie."

I feel fortunate to have been born in America, and I am grateful for having been born in the South. There is no doubt I faced many struggles and tough challenges. But the struggles and challenges I was forced to endure actually instilled within me a belief that I could not only survive against the long odds of segregation's death grip, but also rise to even greater heights. I always hoped the next day would be better than the previous day. Growing up in the South, I had to learn the early lessons of how to identify and avoid dangerous pitfalls. Through it all, I was inspired by my dreams, motivated by hope, and sustained by my faith.

None of us can control the circumstances into which we are born. That is simply the luck of the lottery of life. But it is inexcusable when we allow those circumstances to become shackles that bind or permanent obstacles to achieving and breaking through the glass ceiling. As a youth I dreamed impossible dreams. As an adult, I have lived long enough to see many of those dreams come true and have been blessed to have lived some of my dreams.

I have occasionally been asked if being black and living in the South were barriers to being elected to higher political office such as lieutenant governor or governor. I admit that race and gender are still barriers to be overcome, but neither race nor gender should be used as an excuse for not reaching for a higher rung. Race and gender must never be used as a reason for not trying.

In 1969 I made history and enjoyed a meteoric rise to visibility because I was black. In one magical moment the state of North Carolina, the nation, and the world noticed. A white person being elected mayor of Chapel Hill would not have attracted any attention outside the local community. That electoral event would have certainly not been history-making. Yet there are still those today who believe race and gender are stumbling blocks. I am not one of those people. I believe both can be used as a stepping stone.

There are still uncharted areas to conquer and new vistas to explore. I am optimistic that the future is filled with many breakthrough opportunities. There will eventually be blacks and other minorities elected to the offices of governor. Eventually, electing blacks to the U.S. Senate will become as common as electing blacks to the U.S. House of Representatives. In my early life, I thought it was impossible that a black would ever be elected to the office of President of the United States. At this writing, it is not only possible; it may be imminent. My one regret is that I didn't have the chance to be the one to do it. But, on the other hand, I achieved the breakthrough I was sent to make. I stood on the backs of ancestors long gone and grabbed a higher rung on the ladder of life and pulled myself into the future. I tried to live the Booker T. Washington challenge, "Let your bucket down where you are." Now it's time for me to bend down and lift others up so they can reach the next rung.

Blacks and women have risen to lead great educational institutions, especially in public schools. Blacks are CEOs of major corporations and members of billionaire clubs. I believe it is essential that we celebrate these great achievements and hold them up as symbols of hope for even better days to come. Opportunities for the young are not grounded in dreams, but rather based on real possibilities. Regardless of ethnicity, gender, or socio-economic status, all doors are open to those who are prepared and ready to walk through them. These are role models who can inspire the young and should be held up as symbols of people who are worthy to be emulated.

Any young person expecting to succeed in life must understand the key is education, education, education. I gain great insight from interacting with students and young people and learning about their hopes, dreams and aspirations for their future. Unfortunately, I can discern which students, starting at the fifth grade, are lost, and which ones are rising stars holding on to dreams. In a class of fifteen students, I generally find the class equally divided between those who will graduate from high school and attend college, those who hope to finish high school, and those who don't believe they can go on to higher education and have instead thrown up their hands in despair as they march toward the dropout trap door.

There is no other way to say it, other than to admit there is an educational crisis among black youth. Schools are at a disadvantage trying to motivate black youth because there is a lack of black teachers in classrooms. There are too few male role models, especially black male role models, which enhances the risk that black boys in our state's high schools are an endangered species. The highest rate of dropouts is among black boys. The lack of minority teachers is only a small part of the problem. In too many instances, parental involvement is absent. Community support and engagement is at its lowest level. Can I take on one more challenge to call the broader community to engage with the public school system and help save these kids?

Young people today don't face the same kinds of pitfalls I faced growing up. The pitfalls and potholes young people face today are far more dangerous than the ones I faced. Their pitfalls and potholes are in the form of gangs that engage in threats and intimidation, as the Klan did in my youth. Today's young people face drug dealers who prey on the weakness of their absent fathers, households headed by single mothers, and a dire need for money. Gang leaders become the role models for young people and offer drugs as the next rung on the ladder of success. Therefore, it is imperative that those who have escaped the jaws of poverty and made it out go back and extend a hand of hope to these youth.

I challenge us all to learn from history and never be enslaved by it. I especially challenge adults to step up and become mentors and role models for young people in their community. Every day we live we should find some way to be a symbol of hope for someone else.

Young people and adults must ask and answer the following three questions: "How do I want to be remembered? Do I want to be someone who just occupied a space and when I leave it? Have made no difference? Or do I want to be remembered as someone who built a set of stairs that others could climb to the next level, where they can build a life for themselves, but more importantly leave a set of stairs for the next generation?" I challenge us to occasionally look in the mirror and ask, "Who am I, and why am I really here?"

Youth today are faced with so many choices and are forced to make a multitude of tough decisions. Black youth are especially confused as to which road to travel. Those who dominate their attention are not living the most wholesome lives or presenting the most constructive image. Athletes, entertainers—especially rap artists—and drug dealers are constants in their lives and become the available rung to grab on the ladder. I know that young people today don't need advice as much as they need help to develop a life plan. That's why realistic and accessible positive role models are needed, especially for black males.

I continue to try to be a role model, not necessarily for someone to be like me or to duplicate my achievements. I am a role model to the extent it helps others believe they can achieve and succeed. It is not that people should think they can play basketball like Michael Jordan or hit a golf ball like Tiger Woods, but they should instead believe they should strive to be the best they can be. That's my idea of a role model. A role model isn't necessarily someone who does great things, but rather a person who lives so well that others admire and respect them because of what they stand for, not for what they have achieved.

Minority role models are too scarce, and many of the black men promoted as role models don't exhibit strong character or high moral integrity. The media does not promote positive role models who are black with the same zeal that they promote negative role models. It is essential that young people are exposed to blacks who have succeeded in the fields of academia, business, and politics. That will be the greatest challenge going forward. My mission is to help young blacks and minorities in general realize that more people succeed using their minds than simply relying on their muscles.

As I reflect on my life and the many challenges and disappointments I have experienced, I conclude that barriers are erected in our paths to test our determination. It is our determination that becomes the jackhammer we can use to demolish the obstacles in our path.

Our bodies are only the vessel through which we can bring our true selves to life and express our ideas and thoughts. The vessel is not our life. Our lives will go on, long after the vessel has been stored and is no longer functional.

The first book I ever read from cover to cover in one sitting was one entitled *I Dare You*, by William H. Danforth. This book helped me to see beyond my current circumstances, and accept the challenge to break down barriers in my path. One paragraph that had the greatest impact on me contained a statement by H. G. Wells, who describes how every human being can determine whether he or she has really succeeded in life. He said: "Wealth, notoriety, place, and power are no measure of success whatever. The only true measure of success is the ratio between what we might have done and what we might have been on the one hand, and the thing we have made and the thing we have made of ourselves on the other" (p. 6). The message I got from that statement was that I could control my destiny in spite of the potholes and pitfalls in life. It confirmed my mother's message to me, that I should always do my best. At that moment, I knew the choice would be mine.

There are two diverse actions which will always yield the same results. If you face adversity and become discouraged, throw up your hands in despair and quit, or if you are successful and become happy and inactive— either way you will not progress any further.

Vision is the underpinning of a mission. If you can envision a goal or an objective, then that is the basis upon which you build a mission to pursue. If you stand and look out at the ocean, beyond the horizon is a ship. You don't know where it is, but you have to know there is a ship out there. If you were to try to make contact with that ship, you would go straight toward the horizon and know that at some point you are going to make contact. That is what life is about. We can't always see the ship. We can't always see the end. But we should have a picture in our mind of what the end should be then set out to make it happen.

To me that's what living in the South is all about. I couldn't see the possibility of ever being mayor or ever running for lieutenant governor, but I built on the words that were willed to me by my teacher Mrs. Myrtha Williams: "I can't promise you will ever have an opportunity, but I can guarantee that if an opportunity should ever come you, you will be ready and prepared to seize it."

I have lived all my life in the South. This experience is what has made me who I am. I have been so blessed to have lived such a happy life. In spite of the obstacles and struggles to survive, I was made stronger because I was born and raised in the South. This southern experience positioned me to become a beacon light of hope, a symbol of optimism, and a bulldozer of determination. Today, I can say I am proud to be a Southerner and am very happy that I stayed at home, sacrificed, survived, and made a difference. In the South I developed the strength, determination, and courage to be a leader.

Postscript: I Am a Teacher

I am Challenged to carry on the tradition of those who were teachers through the centuries: Aristotle, Plato, Booker T. Washington, Thomas Jefferson, Daniel Webster, Susan B. Anthony, and Mary McLeod Bethune. I excite my students by asking probing questions and by encouraging them to explore new vistas and share new ideas. I champion the principles of education and am the torch that lights candles of knowledge.

I am a Teacher.

I am a Field General fighting battles to combat enemies of education such as ignorance, apathy, fear, prejudice, peer pressure, and conformity. My combat weapons are intelligence, curiosity, individuality, creativity, faith, love, and the creation of a yearning for knowledge.

I am a Teacher.

I am Different People: an actor, a doctor, a coach, a friend, a psychologist, a lawyer, but most of all I am hope for a better tomorrow. I demand excellence while pushing my students to reach perfection. I work to avoid making mistakes, because my mistakes are released into the world and could become a plague upon society.

I am a Teacher.

I am Powerful Enough to breathe determination into the minds of my students. I plant seeds for new ideas, which I nourish and fertilize with love, truth, curiosity, and creativity so they may grow into trees of knowledge and impact the lives of generations yet unborn.

I am a Teacher.

I am a Miner who digs deep into the minds of my students and discovers a motherlode of talent embedded among the rocks of self-doubt, lack of confidence, confusion, and fear. I do not seek material riches, yet I enjoy great wealth. My value is based on the satisfaction that I have made a difference in the lives of my students.

I am a Teacher.

I am a Role Model for my students. My vision must be so clear that my students can stand beside me and see it for themselves, and, even better, they can create their own visions. I help my students understand that being educated is not just remembering facts, but mastering how to think and learn even when the facts are long forgotten. Inspiring and educating my students is like lighting a fire.

I am a Teacher.

I spend my days shaping the future through the lives of my students. I am a symbol of education, the true hope for a better tomorrow, and a contributor to eternity. I am so blessed, and so lucky, and so proud because **I AM a Teacher.**

Index

Page numbers of black and white photographs are in *italics*. Photographs from the color insert are listed as PLATES.